Language, Music, and Mind

Language, Music, and Mind

Diana Raffman

A Bradford Book
The MIT Press
Cambridge, Massachusetts
London, England

This book was set in Palatino by The MIT Press and was printed and bound in the United States of America.

Library of Congress Cataloging-in-Publication Data

Raffman, Diana.
    Language, music, and mind / Diana Raffman.
       p. cm.
    "A Bradford Book."
    Includes bibliographical references and index.
    ISBN 0-262-18150-9
    1. Music—Philosophy and aesthetics.   2. Music—Psychological aspects.
    3. Music and language.   4. Cognitive psychology.   5. Philosophy of mind.
    I. Title.
    ML3800.R25   1993
    781'.11—dc20   92-26560
                                                                                                                                    CIP
                                                                                                                                    MN

Parts of this book are reprinted from *Language of Art*, by Nelson Goodman, 1968, Hackett Publishing, Indianapolis; from "Quining Qualia" by Daniel Dennett, in *Consciousness and Contemporary Science*, 1988, edited by A. Marcel and E. Bisiach, Oxford University Press, New York; from "The Meaning of Music" by Diana Raffman, in *Midwest Studies in Philosophy, Vol. XVI: Philosophy and the Arts*, © 1991 by University of Notre Dame Press; from *A Generative Theory of Tonal Music* by Fred Lerdahl and Ray Jackendoff, 1983, The MIT Press, Cambridge, © 1983 by MIT; from *The Modularity of Mind* by Jerry A. Fodor, The MIT Press, Cambridge, © 1983 by MIT; and from *Aspects of the Theory of Syntax* by Noam Chomsky, The MIT Press, Cambridge, © 1965 by MIT. All excerpts reprinted by permission.

To Ruth Barcan Marcus

Contents

Preface   ix

Chapter 1
Introduction: The Problem   1

Chapter 2
A Cognitivist Theory of Music Perception   11

Chapter 3
Does Music Mean What It Cannot Say?   37

Chapter 4
A Psychology of Musical Nuance   63

Chapter 5
The Ineffability of Musical Nuance   83

Chapter 6
Naturalizing Nelson Goodman   99

Chapter 7
Qualms About Quining Qualia   125

Notes   147
Bibliography   161
Index   167

Preface

This book is ultimately about a pair of oppositions. The first erects a divide between two kinds of perceptual properties, where by 'perceptual' I mean properties that objects are perceived as having—like colors, textures, pitches, and timbres. (Philosophers often call them 'secondary qualities'.) It turns out that some of these perceptual properties cannot be *remembered*. For example, we cannot remember—in the sense of being able to re-identify or recognize by inspection (e.g., by looking)— precise colors. We can remember red and blue, even scarlet and indigo, as such, but we cannot remember precise *shades* of red and blue. In more traditional philosophical terms, we can remember the determinables (viz., the general categories) but not their determinates (viz., the finest values we can discriminate within those categories). Similarly, we can remember augmented fourths and major sixths as such, but not the specific "determinate" intervals we can discriminate within those general interval categories.

The second opposition has to do with what we can and cannot *say*. Not surprisingly, learning a word for a property one perceives requires that one remember the property (in the recognitional sense at issue); for example, learning to call major sixths 'major sixths', by listening, requires that one remember what a major sixth sounds like. Hence if there are perceptual properties that cannot be remembered, then there are perceptual properties that cannot be reported on the basis of inspection; for example, although we can report that a sound is a major sixth on the basis of listening to it, we cannot report that it is this or that particular *determinate* major sixth.

I suspect that this allied pair of oppositions—between what we can and cannot remember, on the one hand, and what we can and cannot say, on the other—lies close to the heart of such varied issues as the possibility of a private language, the psychological plausibility of eliminative materialism about the mind-brain, and the metaphysical status of secondary qualities. I do not discuss those topics here, however. Here I examine the relationship between memory and verbalization as it figures in the perception of tonal music. Specifically, I invoke recent psychological theories of perceptual memory and language processing in order to shed light on the traditional philosophical problem of ineffable musical knowledge. Philosophers of art have long written of musical knowledge that cannot be put into words; I formulate a psychologically plausible account of its content and etiology in terms of the pair of oppositions just described. My hope is that, in addition to illuminating an old philosophical puzzle, the present work carves out a new approach to problems in aesthetics—an approach that augments traditional "aprioristic" treatments with the explanatory power and empirical testability of contemporary cognitive science.

Because the view advanced here draws upon research in a variety of fields, I have many people to thank. My first and greatest debt is to the philosopher Ruth Marcus, whose wisdom, erudition, and unblinking intellectual courage were a beacon throughout the project's history. Any virtues of the present work owe largely to conversations with her. Ivan Fox and Robert Kraut influenced my philosophical thinking at each step of the way, and Jamshed Bharucha and Mari Riess Jones taught me virtually everything I know about the psychology of music. Sensitive readings by those just named, and also by philosophers William Lycan, Michael Watkins, and Donald Hubin, vastly improved the manuscript in both substance and style. In addition, I have benefitted from the insights and criticisms of Cy Anders, Brad Armendt, Dirk Baltzly, Robert Batterman, Simon Blackburn, David Blinder, Steven Boer, Jim Bogen, Phillip Bricker, Lee Brown, Daniel Dennett, Jill Dieterle, Daniel Farrell, Pieranna Garavaso, Jody Graham, Karsten Harries, Terry Horgan, Jonathan Lear, George Pappas, Barbara Scholz, George Schumm, Stewart Shapiro, Ted Uehling, Jefferson White, and Andrew Woodfield in philosophy; Jack Baird, Robert Crowder, Gary Kidd, Lester Krueger, Caroline Palmer, and John Sloboda in psychology; David Butler, Rita LaPlante, Fred Lerdahl, Nancy Raffman, and Relly Raffman in music; Peter Culicover, Mike Geis, Robert Levine, and Craige Roberts in linguistics; and also audiences at Denison University,

Franklin and Marshall College, Ohio State University, the University of Cincinnati, the University of Minnesota at Morris, the International Conference on Naturalized Epistemology and Philosophy of Mind (Dubrovnik, 1989), the Conference on Cognitive Bases of Musical Communication (Ohio State University, 1990), and the 15th Annual Meeting of the Society for Philosophy and Psychology (Tucson, 1989), where portions of the book were read in one form or another. Michael Aronson, Angela Blackburn, Alex Holzman, Eve LaPlante, and Virgina LaPlante provided excellent editorial advice at various stages of the publication process.

A good deal of the material contained in chapter 5 appeared in an earlier paper, "Toward A Cognitive Theory of Musical Ineffability" (*Review of Metaphysics* 41, June 1988, 685-706); chapter 3 is a considerably expanded and revised version of a paper called "The Meaning of Music" (*Midwest Studies in Philosophy*, Volume XVI, *Philosophy and the Arts* 1991, 360-377 [University of Notre Dame Press]); and some of the material contained in chapter 6 is based on arguments presented in a paper "Goodman, Density, and the Limits of Sense Perception" (*The Interpretation of Music: Philosophical Essays*, Krausz [ed.], forthcoming [Oxford University Press]). I am grateful to The Review of Metaphysics, University of Notre Dame Press, and Oxford University Press for permission to reprint.

Finally, I thank Harry Stanton for the privilege of publishing this work with Bradford Books, Senior Editor Katherine Arnoldi for her meticulous reading of the manuscript, and Bradford Coordinating Editor Teri Mendelsohn for her unfailingly cheerful and patient management.

Language, Music, and Mind

Chapter 1

Introduction: The Problem

[W]orks of art are objects of the sort that can only be known in sensing. . . .
*[O]ne may wish to say [that] seeing feels like knowing. . . . In such cases,
knowing functions like an organ of sense. . . . Such objects are only* known
by feeling, or in feeling....[T]he result is one of knowledge. . . . This seems
to me to suggest why one is anxious to communicate the experience of such
objects. . . . It is not merely that I want to tell you how it is with me, how I
feel. . . . It's rather that I want to tell you something I've seen, or heard, or
realized, or come to understand, for the reasons for which* such *things are
communicated (because it is news, about a world we share, or could). Only
I find that I can't tell you. I want to tell you because the knowledge, unshared,
is a burden. . . . [U]nless I can tell what I know, there is a suggestion . . . that
I do* not *know. But I do—what I see is* that *(pointing to the object). But for
that to communicate, you have to see it too.*

Stanley Cavell 1967, 78–80

*[I]t seems peculiarly difficult for our literal minds to grasp the idea that
anything can be* known *which cannot be* named....*But this...is really the
strength of musical expressiveness: that* music articulates the forms that
language cannot set forth....*The imagination that responds to music is
personal and associative and logical, tinged with affect, tinged with bodily
rhythm, tinged with dream, but* concerned *with a wealth of formulations for
its wealth of wordless knowledge.*

Susanne Langer 1942, 198, 207

If all meanings could be adequately expressed by words, the arts of painting and music would not exist. There are values and meanings that can be expressed only by immediately visible and . . . audible qualities, and to ask what they mean in the sense of something that can be put into words is to deny their distinctive existence.

John Dewey 1934, 74

Despite considerable differences in ideology, objective, and style, these theorists join in giving voice to one of the most deeply rooted convictions in modern aesthetics: our knowledge of artworks is, in some essential respect, ineffable.[1] In apprehending a work of art, we come to know something we cannot put into words.

Convictions widely shared usually admit a good deal of variation, and this one is no exception. Is it that the content of our ineffable knowledge defies verbalization altogether, or that it cannot be *exhausted* by verbal report? Is it that there could be no terms for it, or that even if there were such terms, we would not be able to apply them? Musical ineffability, the subject of discussion here, is often associated with the character of our affective experience. We are told, for example, that music symbolizes human feelings; and feelings can be known only *by* feeling. Here again we find diversity of opinion in matters of detail: does a piece of music express or evoke these feelings? Or does it somehow embody them? Are the relevant feelings stereotypical emotions, like anger and joy, or are they peculiarly musical feelings? And so on.

The works cited above strike a deep truth about music—we find ourselves there, as the saying goes. At the same time, they leave something to be desired. Like much "traditional" philosophical writing on the subject, it seems to me, these works *describe* our ineffable knowledge but do not adequately *explain* it. Things are stirred about in interesting and attractive ways, yet many of the initial questions remain, as though we had twirled in place.[2]

What sort of explanation would satisfy us? Consider: 'What is an artwork?' 'Are the intentions of the artist relevant to an interpretation of his work?' 'Do artworks have an ethical function?' In the main, questions like these are fodder for conceptual analysis. By contrast, questions about musical ineffability are (at least in part) questions about the nature of musical *experience,* a real-time psychological process: it is supposedly *in hearing* a musical work that we acquire ineffable knowledge. If that is so, then there is every reason to expect that the sciences of psychology and psycholinguistics, among others, will be relevant to our understanding here. To put it simply, I want to see how these empirical disciplines might explain the apparent fact that conscious musical experience gives rise to claims of ineffable knowledge: from a psychological point of view, what goes on in music perception that could plausibly be described as the acquisition of knowledge that cannot be put into words? My goal is not to replace the traditional philosophical accounts but rather to augment them—indeed, in many instances, to vindicate them—with a psychological theory. The present story is complementary, not subversive.

Certainly there are those who have recognized the need for psychological theory in the philosophy of music,[3] but to my mind they have not followed through. That our forebears should disappoint in this respect is hardly surprising, for only recently has a *bona fide* psychology of music been available. Music theorists have long supposed that musical experience and behavior are systematically related to structural regularities in heard pieces, but only with the advent of so-called cognitivist theorizing have the psychologists appropriated music perception as an object of scientific study. Cognitivism, a theoretical approach embracing recent work in the philosophy of mind, linguistics, artificial intelligence, and psychology, among others, is motivated in large measure by the idea that many of our psychological processes are computations defined over mental symbols or "representations."[4] According to the cognitive psychologists, listeners unconsciously abstract and store structural information from the music they hear, thereby establishing longstanding mental representations that shape their subsequent music perception. It is presumably on account of this reciprocity of musical and mental structure that a special psychology of music could be developed.[5]

My aims are three. First I shall develop a cognitivist explanation of musical ineffability; this is the project of chapters 2 through 5. In drafting such an account it will be important to keep in mind that musical knowledge, ineffable or otherwise, is perceptual knowledge: any story we tell will be at bottom a story about (auditory) perception.

I shall try to show that when the problem of musical ineffability is planted squarely in the perceptual arena, it can be illuminated by the adoption of a recent cognitivist theory of perception (Fodor 1983) in conjunction with a generative grammar for tonal music (Lerdahl and Jackendoff 1983). On this two-headed view, conscious musical perception or experience results from the unconscious computation of a series of increasingly abstract mental representations of an acoustic signal. Our task will be to discover where in this multileveled scheme any ineffabilities might reside.

Three candidates emerge. The first, which I call *structural ineffability*, results from limitations on the listener's access to his underlying representations of musical structure. Although the content of these representations is systematically reflected in his conscious auditory experience, he cannot always *say* what that content is (i.e., which musical structures are represented). To that extent, I suggest, he has conscious but ineffable musical knowledge. The second ineffability, *feeling ineffability*, derives from the sensory-perceptual or "felt" character of musical knowledge. Here the familiar thought is that musical knowledge requires (actual, occurrent) sense-perception of musical stimuli at some point in its etiology and is to that extent ineffable: it cannot be communicated entirely by language. Of the three ineffabilities, this second owes least to the cognitivist framework *per se*; it is revealed largely by conceptual analysis and should be acknowledged, I think, in *any* theory of musical ineffability, cognitivist or otherwise.

I shall not devote much attention to these first two candidates, since from a philosophical point of view they are less significant than the third. This last, the heart of our theory, results from the absence of certain categorial structures at early ("shallow") levels in the listener's series of representations of the musical signal. It turns out that certain features of the music, often called 'nuances', are likely to be recovered so early in the representational process that they fail to be mentally categorized or type-identified in the manner thought necessary for verbal report. As a result, the listener is consciously aware of the nuances but cannot say which nuances they are. Therein lies their *nuance ineffability*.

My second aim is to consider our cognitivist theory of musical ineffability in light of some well-known traditional treatments of the problem, principally those of Cavell and Nelson Goodman (1968), in order to see how far the *avant-garde* squares with the old guard while making good on its explanatory promises. Calling this part of the project 'second' suggests that it follows the theory of ineffability, but in fact my exchanges with Cavell are marbled through the third and fifth chapters. In chapter 6, Goodman's account of musical ineffability is gratifyingly "rediscovered and vindicated by cognitive science";[6] indeed, it may turn out that his theory of artistic symbolism is *rescued* by our cognitivist story. In a nutshell, Goodman's analysis requires the theoretical possibility of a dense ordering of values along musical dimensions like pitch and loudness—that is, the theoretical possibility of an infinite number of pitches and dynamic levels so ordered that between any two there is a third. True to the theoretical asceticism for which he is well known, Goodman is apparently oblivious to the strain such a requirement places on the *perceptual* nature of the values involved,[7] and his analysis may suffer as a result. Happily, our cognitivist account affords a way to preserve the central insight of Goodman's view while respecting the finitude of human perception.

Although it departs the specifically musical arena, chapter 7 is in many respects the most important chapter in the book, for it testifies to the import of our musical reflections for issues central to the study of mind. In particular, our account of the nuance ineffability casts doubt upon a certain prominent theory of consciousness. Philosophers and psychologists alike have long taken for granted the existence of a special tie between conscious awareness and verbal expression; as Jerry Fodor observes, "the criterion of accessibility [is standardly supposed to be] availability for explicit report" (1983, 56). Recently, however, Daniel Dennett has vaulted the standard view to new heights: consciousness, he declares, just *consists in* a sequence of "propositional episodes" or "intentions-to-say-that-p," whose contents are by their very nature exhaustively reportable (1979, 1982, e.g.; see also chapter 7, note 1). My third aim, and the project of chapter 7, is to show that the nuance ineffability of certain shallow mental representations poses a threat to Dennett's propositionalist program. In particular, if the theory propounded below is correct, then some sensory-perceptual states have contents—and I mean legitimate representational contents—that are consciously accessible but not reportable. In such cases, *contra* Dennett, saying what one experiences is (psychologically) impossible.

I suppose an introduction is the place for policy statements. Here are an unavoidable few.

1. First, I shall follow Cavell and Langer (among others) in taking the ineffability at issue to be a property of (some of) our *knowledge:* ineffable knowledge will be conscious knowledge that cannot be communicated (or communicated exhaustively) in words. Some are inclined to call the objects of knowledge, as opposed to the knowledge itself, ineffable, as in 'The subject matter of this painting is ineffable' or 'Human feelings are ineffable'; but these ways of talking are usually elliptical for claims of ineffable *knowledge* (of the subject matter or the feelings, for example). Similarly, I shall sometimes speak of features of the music as being ineffable, but that too will be short for talk about the knowledge of those features.[8]

There are places in the philosophical literature, of course, where something is said to be ineffable and *un*knowable. As William Kennick (1967) observes, Kantian things-in-themselves are a case in point: strictly speaking, about these nothing can be said *or known*. Also, and trivially, as effability goes, so goes knowability on any view that holds the two bound together in principle (a typical positivist view, for example). The success of our undertaking here, however, will depend on a divorce of knowing from saying; we seek to exhibit something the listener consciously knows but cannot report. Such a strategy sits well with standard philosophical usage:

> The ineffable must not be confused with the unknowable. One may assert ... that some things are both ineffable and unknowable; nevertheless, the concept of the ineffable is usually so construed that it makes sense to say, "I know something somehow, but I cannot put it into words; I cannot say what I know" (Kennick 1967, 181).

Just what ineffable musical knowledge comes to on a cognitivist account will emerge as we go along, but two brief points are worth making here. First, for the time being I shall help myself to the cognitivist's conception of knowledge as mental representation of some kind: knowing a piece of music, for example, will consist (at least partly) in having a certain sort of mental representation in your head. Second, whatever its precise nature proves to be, the sort of knowledge at issue will be a lot more like "perceptual," than like "propositional" or "descriptive," knowledge.[9]

2. Although the extension of 'ineffable musical knowledge' remains to be discovered, I shall stipulate this much: I shall not call 'ineffable' what cannot be verbalized on account of, say, lack of musical training or ignorance of a certain vocabulary. For example, the listener unable to say whether a musical passage is in simple or compound meter, or a triad in first or second inversion, does not therefore have ineffable knowledge of those phenomena. The sorts of ineffability at issue here, we shall find, involve rather more insurmountable "inabilities." Let me emphasize furthermore that, despite the optimistic tenor of the plan outlined above, I do not pretend to offer an exhaustive account of musical ineffability, or even of those ineffabilities that arise in a cognitivist musical framework; no doubt there is more to the story than what I say here. Rather, I mean simply to explore *some* of the ways in which cognitive scientific theory and methodology might be brought to bear on the problem.

3. In the chapters that follow, I shall often employ the case of musical pitch as my exemplar; and as any philosopher of music is well aware, the metaphysics of pitch (among other musical dimensions) is a topic beset by the confusions and inconsistencies characteristic of the literature on secondary qualities generally. In particular, are pitches properties of tones (sounds, acoustic stimuli), and thus in some sense "objective," or are they properties of our perceptions of those tones, and thus in some sense "subjective"? Or a cross between the two? Or none of these? The following passages, from prominent works in psychology and psychophysics, are indicative:

> Pitch may be defined as that attribute of auditory sensation in terms of which sounds may be ordered on a musical scale. In other words, pitch is that attribute the variation of which constitutes melody. . . . The pitch of a sound is related to its repetition rate and, hence, in the case of a sine wave, to frequency. It should be emphasized that pitch is a subjective property of a stimulus, and as such cannot be measured directly (Moore 1977, 17).

> The actual 'pitch' (the subjective sensation of frequency) of the tones . . . is perceived normally as being a function of the 'fundamental' [frequency] (Davies 1978, 31).

> Pitch is that qualitative attribute of auditory sensation which de-
> notes highness or lowness in the musical scale and is conditioned
> primarily on the frequency of sound waves. . . . [Pitch] is the mental
> and musical correlate of the frequency of the vibrations which
> constitute the physical tone. . . . [W]e can never be directly aware
> of the rate of vibration as such, for we hear it as musical pitch. This
> is one of the wondrous transformations 'from matter to mind'
> (Seashore 1967, 53).

Since the provision of a thoroughgoing metaphysics of pitch would
require a book in itself, and since in any case we need not resolve the
metaphysical issue here and now, I shall for present purposes simply
assume the following: whatever else they may be, pitches are properties
that tones are heard (mentally represented) as having; if you like,
pitches are properties ascribed to tones in auditory perception by
normal observers under normal listening conditions (whatever those
are). Accordingly, my talk about the pitches of tones, or about pitches
per se, will be elliptical for talk about properties that tones are heard
as having; and my talk of hearing or perceiving pitches will be elliptical
for talk of hearing tones as having certain pitches. (Just which pitch a
tone is heard as having is largely—though not entirely—a function of
the tone's frequency; see chapter 2, note 9.) Furthermore, in referring
to the mental states that represent heard tones as having certain pitches,
I shall often say that those states represent (or are representations of) those
pitches; but the latter way of talking will be elliptical for the former. Thus
whatever exactly the metaphysics of pitch may be, it makes essential
appeal to the (auditory) mental representations of normal listeners; in
this sense at least, pitches are perceptual properties. That much I shall
take for granted throughout. Beyond what I have said here, an intuitive grasp of the notion of musical pitch should suffice for present
purposes.

4. As must by now be clear, I do not stint in helping myself to other
people's theories—for instance, Fodor's theory of perceptual input
systems, the Lerdahl-Jackendoff musical grammar, John Anderson's
propositional network (1980), and a number of cognitive psychological
theories of music processing. To boot, I help myself to these accounts
more or less unexamined: I propose neither to criticize nor to defend
them, although naturally a bit of both will go on in the course of things.
My aim, rather, is to show that if we adopt these cognitivist approaches,

a philosophically and psychologically well-heeled account of musical ineffability is forthcoming. In particular, I shall remain neutral with regard to the controversy between so-called classical computational theories of mind (like Fodor's) and the new Parallel Distributed Processing models. As it happens, most of the research germane to our investigation is cast in the classical mold, but I shall appeal to some relevant work in the connectionist (PDP) literature as well (see, e.g., Bharucha 1987a,b and §4.2). In any case, so far as I can see, nothing essential to my view rests upon the special features of either paradigm.

5. Although I have cited, and will from time to time continue to cite, philosophical claims about other artforms or the arts in general, the theory presented here is intended to apply exclusively to music.[10] It seems to me that the various arts are more different than they are alike, and the artistic biases of aestheticians all too often result in forced applications of theory to unwilling media. In the interest of avoiding *ad hoc* theoretical generalizations, and, more importantly, because at least some of the psychological structures to which I shall appeal are thought to be special to musical processing, my conclusions are restricted accordingly.[11] If they turn out to apply to other artforms, so much the better.

6. A topic of central importance and heated debate in contemporary philosophy of mind is the existence of *qualia*, the supposed "phenomenological" characteristics or "raw feels" of our conscious sensory-perceptual and somatic states. While I have no intention of entering the fray here, I want to acknowledge straightaway that the ineffability standardly ascribed to qualia, whatever its metaphysical standing, may be partly or even wholly what some philosophers of art have had in mind in speaking of the ineffability of our musical knowledge. I shall return to the topic of qualia in chapter 7 in connection with Dennett's program, but for now I am going to set the issue aside. Instead, I shall be occupied with the aforementioned trio of ineffabilities which arise in a cognitivist framework, and which should, it seems to me, be countenanced by friend and foe of qualia alike.

7. I envision, and would like my reader to envision, the development of a theory of musical ineffability as a starting place rather than a goal. Taken by itself, the theory occupies a small corner of a small province of philosophy; its real significance lies in its wider import. By the end,

I hope to have shown at least the following two things. First, that cognitive science is rich in implications for the philosophy of art. The border between psychology and the philosophy of mind is already richly planted; hence insofar as aesthetics makes its home in the latter discipline it is high time for scientific theory to be applied there as well. The philosopher George Dickie insists that scientific psychology has nothing to offer aesthetics: "I am convinced that the problem of the description of the nature of aesthetic experience is not a task to which the techniques of empirical science are relevant" (1961, 302). The present work will, I think, show otherwise. Second, aesthetics sometimes endures a kind of second-class citizenship in philosophy. Though this is not the place to speculate on the reasons for the snub, I do hope to show that reflection on a problem in the philosophy of art can illuminate the nature of mentality generally, and in a manner respectable by the standards of scientific psychology and philosophy of mind. If cognitive science has much to say to aesthetics, aesthetics has plenty to say in return.

8. Lastly, I must prevail upon my reader to bear in mind the diversity of the audience to which this book is addressed. In developing an account of musical ineffability I have drawn upon theoretical and experimental work in psychology, psychoacoustics, linguistics, psycholinguistics, music theory, and the philosophies of mind, art, and language; and my intended readership includes scholars in these various disciplines. In order to keep the discussion accessible to such an eclectic bunch, I shall need to provide rather more in the way of "background" exposition (and, in places, more notes and quotes) than is customary in an original theoretical work; to some extent, any reader will find the discussion alternately remedial and arcane. I have tried to keep the didactic sections as simple and as brief as possible, but there is no avoiding them entirely.

So much for the preliminaries. Let us turn now to the first element of a cognitive theory of musical ineffability—the psychology of music perception.[12]

Chapter 2
A Cognitivist Theory of Music Perception

An analogy to language may not be out of place here. Just as one can tease apart a series of levels of language—from the basic phonological level, through a sensitivity to word order and word meaning, to the ability to appreciate larger entities, like stories—so, too, in the realm of music, it is possible to examine sensitivity to individual tones or phrases, but also to look at how these fit together into larger musical structures...

Howard Gardner 1983, 108.

2.1 Fodor's Theory of Input Systems

In his seminal book *The Modularity of Mind* (1983), Jerry Fodor has detailed what he calls "the establishment view," a.k.a. "the inferential view," of perception.[1] As Fodor sees it, the *raison d'être* of perception is to make the external environment accessible to central cognitive systems like belief, memory, and decision-making—in short, to render the world accessible to thought. Perception begins when that world impinges on the sense organs or transducers (the retina and basilar membrane, among others). However, whereas the transducers respond to stimulation by the likes of electromagnetic wavelengths and acoustic frequencies, our beliefs and memories and decisions are about ice cubes and faces and doorbells; in Fodor's terms, whereas the transducers deliver representations of proximal stimulation patterns, central processes typically operate on representations of distal objects as such. So the question is: how do we get from the former to the latter, from mental representations "couched in the vocabulary" of proximal stimulations to mental representations (viz. perceptions) couched in the vocabulary of ice cubes and doorbells?

Fodor fills this categorial lacuna with what he calls *input systems*—psychological mechanisms whose function is to interpret transducer outputs in a form that central processing can understand. That's *interpret*, not *translate*, Fodor emphasizes, for whereas translation preserves content, the transformations by the input systems do not: representations of retinal excitations are not informationally equivalent to representations of ice cubes, no matter how readily the latter may "follow" from the former.[2] The brand of interpretation at issue consists in a series of so-called nondemonstrative inferences that "have as their 'premises' transduced representations of proximal stimulus configurations, and as their 'conclusions' representations of the character and distribution of distal objects" (42). Fodor's thought is that since the transducers are sensitive solely to properties of proximal stimuli and, unlike the input systems, effect no transformations of the information they import, higher level representations of the distal world must be constructed or *inferred* from the transducer outputs.[3] What you have, then, is a tripartite scheme of transducers, input systems, and central cognitive systems, corresponding roughly to the traditional triptych of sensation, perception, and cognition.

Exactly what sort of nondemonstrative inference *is* this? On its face it seems a far cry from familiar cases involving ravens and emeralds, but in fact it is not so different. Perhaps the first thing to say about this species of inference is that it isn't something *we* do; it is something some of our "sub-personal" *parts* do. Which sub-personal parts? *Ex hypothesi* the input systems. Second, perceptual inference is computationally defined. This means that the mechanisms that perform the inferences have access only to the *formal* (as opposed to *semantic* or *contentful*) properties of the mental representations in which the perceptual information is couched.[4] As a first approximation, an input process is a series of computations yielding a representation of the environment in a format that central processes, also computational, can read.[5]

Since the crudest illustrations are often the clearest, let me flesh out the picture in this very crude way. (I shall keep to the visual story for now, since it is the most familiar, but analogous accounts are envisioned for the other input systems as well.) Perceptual processing commences with the stimulation of the visual transducer (the retina) by ambient light. Each of the stimulated retinal cells "responds" that it's being stimulated at such-and-such an intensity, the totality of these responses being said to represent the pattern of causative proximal stimulations. Subsequent tiers of neurons then "read" the transducer output and, from that "premise," "infer" or "hypothesize" what the distal source of the stimulations is. Suppose a given tier of post-transductive neurons are edge detectors. In that case the "hypothesis" they compute will specify the location and orientation of the object's edges. In this way, more or less successive tiers of neurons infer that the distal object has such-and-such texture gradients, such-and-such edges, such-and-such a shape, etc., and finally that it is a such-and-such—an ice cube, say.[6] In sum, the transducers tell the input systems what the pattern of proximal stimulations is, and on that basis the input systems tell central processing what they "think" the distal object is.[7]

Central systems do not in general have access to the contents of intermediate (i.e., "pre-perceptual") levels in the representational series computed by an input processor. This is not to suggest, however, that all information retrieved at shallower levels is lost to central processes (nor, in particular, to conscious awareness); although some very shallow representations may be entirely off limits, when you consciously see an ice cube you consciously see its edges and shape *inter alia*. Rather, Fodor's point is that central systems have no access to the content of shallower levels taken, as it were, *simpliciter*. Crudely: you can't see an ice cube *simply* as an assembly of edges; on the contrary, you can't help seeing it *as* a cube of ice.

None of the foregoing is meant to identify the input systems with the standard five senses. Instead, Fodor conceives these inferential processors as individuated "within (and, quite possibly, across) the traditional modes" (47). In particular, one of his principal contentions is that the mechanisms which process speech stimuli also constitute an input system. While the perceptual input systems issue in proprietary representations of ice cubes and doorbells, the language processor delivers structural (viz. grammatical, and probably also logical) analyses of heard utterances. The inferences that generate these analyses are likely to range over acoustic, phonological, lexical, and syntactic representations:

> Sentence comprehension...involves not only acoustic encoding but also the recovery of phonetic and lexical content and syntactic form

(56)....Understanding a token sentence presumably involves assigning it a structural description...and that is precisely the sort of
function we would expect an input system to perform (44).

We shall hear more about the linguistic input system as we go along.

No doubt input processing is vastly more baroque than this thumb-
nail sketch would suggest, involving myriad feedback loops, complex
pattern recognition, feature detection, and schemata of all sorts. Moreover, for the most part we shall not even be considering Fodor's
principal thesis in *The Modularity of Mind,* which is that the input
systems, as opposed to central systems like belief and memory, are
modular—that is, domain-specific, hardwired, informationally encap-
sulated mechanisms (mental reflexes, if you like) designed for the
"stupid" but speedy import of information about the distal environment.[8] For our purposes, the important point will be that perception
proceeds via the computation of a series of mental representations,
beginning with transducer outputs and culminating in the perception
of an object in the world. The categories mobilized—you might say: the
ontic commitments made—at relatively deeper (higher, later) levels in
the series are more *abstract* than those mobilized at shallower levels.
The category 'ice cube' is more abstract, in this sense, than the category
'vertical edge'; the category 'noun phrase' is more abstract than the
category 'vowel'; and as we shall see, the category 'melody' is more
abstract than the category 'tritone'.

I indicated in chapter 1 that Fodor's program could shed light on the
nature of ineffable musical knowledge insofar as the latter is a kind of
perceptual knowledge. How would a Fodor-type story of music perception go?

First we shall need some plausible candidates for the various levels
of representation of the musical stimulus. At the shallow end, we can
count on the transduction of acoustic features like the frequency and
intensity of the tones. Representations of the so-called *psychoacoustic
correlates* to frequency and intensity—namely pitch and loudness[9]—
are then presumably inferred in parallel from the transducer outputs
(see again note 6). Temporal information about the durations of events
is also sure to be processed at a relatively shallow level, thus enabling
the recovery of the stimulus as a sequence of *pitch-time events* (a.k.a.

notes).[10] But then what? Surely when we hear a piece of music we hear more than a jumble of undifferentiated events. We hear phrases, themes, syncopations, suspensions, tonic chords, cadences and more. What sorts of mental representations underlie this kaleidoscopic richness of musical experience? *Mirabile dictu* we have available a model of music perception that fits neatly into Fodor's multileveled paradigm and hence can provide some plausible answers. The remainder of this chapter will be taken up primarily with an exposition of the musical theory and a discussion of some of the respects in which it evinces the hallmark features of Fodor's input systems. With this theoretical framework in place, we shall be well positioned to introduce two of the three varieties of ineffable musical knowledge cited at the outset.

2.2 Grammars for Language and Music

In his book *Frames of Mind* (1983), Howard Gardner speculates:

> Buried far back in evolution, music and language may have arisen from a common expressive medium (98). . . . Many scholars suspect that linguistic and musical expression and communication had common origins and, in fact, split off from one another several hundred thousand, or perhaps even a million, years ago (115).

The idea that music and language might share a distant ancestry has recently been fueled by the musical application of techniques borrowed from standard Chomskian linguistics. Perhaps the most persuasive and thoroughgoing proposal is the generative grammar for tonal music developed by theorist-composer Fred Lerdahl and linguist Ray Jackendoff.[11] Although there is no evidence of strict or substantive musical analogues to the linguistic ranks of syntax, semantics, and phonology,[12] the *point* of the musical theory is very like that of its linguistic cousin—viz., to model the "largely unconscious knowledge which the [experienced] listener brings to music and which allows him to organize musical sounds into coherent patterns" (1977, 111). The experienced listener—a musical analogue to Chomsky's ideal speaker-hearer—is one familiar with an idiom but not necessarily schooled in its theory. For example, he can recognize novel pieces as tonal, identify various errors of composition and performance, and recognize struc-

tural features like themes and cadences; that is to say, he can "compre-
hend a piece within the idiom" (1983, 3).[13]

Let me begin by sketching the Chomskian background against which
the musical theory is set. Though Lerdahl and Jackendoff rightly insist
that the music-language parallel should not be forced, understanding
their project requires some familiarity with its theoretical heritage.

2.2.1 Linguistic Roots

Chomsky argues that innate linguistic knowledge is required for the
learning of a first language and for linguistic creativity. No inductive
paradigm can explain first language acquisition, he contends, given the
"poverty of the stimulus" to which the novitiate is exposed: acquaintance with a relatively small and often degenerate sample of utterances
cannot by itself account for the speed and generality of the child's
language mastery. Similarly, induction from a corpus of heard sentences cannot explain the competent speaker-hearer's linguistic creativity—that is, his ability to produce and understand indefinitely many
novel sentences. Rather, some antecedent mental structure is required.
According to standard Chomskian theory,[14] the normal human innately
"cognizes" certain universal and general constraints on the character
of possible grammars for natural language. (For example, any such
grammar will have four components—a lexicon and phonological,
syntactic, and semantic rules.) In first language acquisition, these tacit
principles guide the speaker-hearer in the unconscious formulation of
a set of rules (a *generative grammar*) for his particular natural language
(English, or French, or Chinese, or whatever). The formulation of the
grammar is triggered by exposure to heard utterances and subsequently tested against that input. Once the grammatical rules are in
place, they prescribe which of indefinitely many novel utterances are
well-formed or "grammatical" and, hence, understandable.

Despite Lerdahl and Jackendoff's admonition against the drawing of
strict musical analogies, the Chomskian inspiration for the musical
theory is perhaps best appreciated by way of a comparison with the
syntactic rules of the linguistic grammar (hereafter, the "L-grammar").
These latter include recursive phrase structure rules and transformation rules whose specific content is, as I indicated above, variable across
natural languages. The phrase structure rules serve to "rewrite" gram-

matical symbols at each succeeding level in a hierarchical derivation, culminating in a string of terminal symbols (e.g., words) which cannot be further rewritten. In English, 'S' (for 'sentence') might be rewritten as 'NP⌢VP' (for 'noun phrase concatenated with verb phrase'), 'VP' perhaps in turn as 'V⌢NP' ('verb concatenated with noun phrase'), and so on until a terminal string is reached. For a simple example, consider the derivation shown in the phrase marker in figure 2.1 (Chomsky 1965, 65). *Very* roughly, transformation rules are then applied to the phrase marker shown in the figure in order to derive the phrase marker for an actual sentence that may be, say, passive or interrogative. The phrase marker displaying the derivation of the terminal string, together with the phrase marker displaying the derivation of the sentence itself from the terminal string, constitutes the *structural description* of the sentence. Insofar as the grammar generates every well-formed English sentence with its structural description(s),[15] it is said to model syntactic *competence* for English. That is, it models the unconscious syntactic knowledge that (partially) underwrites the ideal speaker-hearer's ability to produce and understand indefinitely many grammatical sentences of his language.[16]

The term 'generative' may suggest that the (mere) enumeration of well-formed strings is of central importance in the linguistic theory. But in fact what is really of interest, in linguistics and music alike, is the structure assigned to those strings. Lerdahl and Jackendoff explain that "despite the term 'generative', the goal in linguistic theory is to find the rules that assign correct structures to sentences. Consequently the sentences as such in linguistic theorizing are usually taken as given" (1983, 112). The musical theory, too, is conceived in this way:

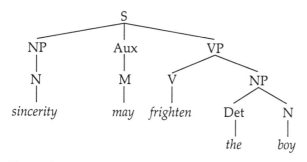

Figure 2.1
Phrase marker from Chomsky, *Aspects of the Theory of Syntax* (1965, 65)

The same holds for our theory of music. It is not intended to enumerate what pieces are possible, but to specify a *structural description* for any tonal piece; that is, the structure that the experienced listener infers in his hearing of the piece (6). . . . Overall, the system can be thought of as taking a given musical surface as input and producing the structure that the listener hears as output (11). . . . [O]ur strategy is amenable to experimental methods in cognitive psychology, in which subjects are typically given a "stimulus object" (such as the musical surface of an existing piece) to which they react under controlled conditions (112).

Although the linguistic structural descriptions are meant to specify the syntactic structures mobilized in production and understanding alike, a conception of the syntactic rules as an "input-output" device assigning structures to antecedently given strings is of course *intuitively* closer to understanding than to production. This proves convenient for Lerdahl and Jackendoff, whose musical model applies only to perception ("understanding"), and not to composition ("production").[17] Indeed, an input-output model of competence might well pave the way for a real-time processing or *performance* model of understanding. That is just what happens in the musical case, to which we now turn.

2.2.2 The Lerdahl-Jackendoff Grammar for Tonal Music

Like its linguistic counterpart, the musical grammar (the "M-grammar") models an underlying *competence*. That is, it models "the largely unconscious knowledge (the 'musical intuition') that the listener brings to his hearing—a knowledge that enables him to organize and make coherent the surface patterns of pitch, attack, duration, intensity, timbre, and so forth" (1983, 3).[18] This knowledge is captured in a set of rules for assigning certain analyses, "structural descriptions," to incoming musical strings. Those strings that admit the right sort of analysis are the ones the listener "understands." On this view, the understanding of a piece of music is a constructive enterprise presupposing a system of mental representation in which such a structural analysis can be carried out. As the authors explain,

[t]here is much more to music than the raw uninterpreted physical signal. . . . [O]ne must . . . treat . . . these kinds of structure . . . as mental products imposed on or inferred from the physical sig-

nal. . . . [A] piece of music is a mentally constructed entity (1983, 4–5).[19]

The metaphysical status of the musical work is, of course, a vexed issue, and I don't propose to take it on at this juncture (although I shall make a few remarks in §2.4). What concerns us at present is rather the idea that music perception or understanding is a constructive representational process.

The idea is roughly this. You, the experienced listener, have unconscious knowledge of certain rules for musical analysis. As you hear an incoming musical signal, you unconsciously represent it and analyze it according to those rules; that is to say, you assign it a structural description. *Ex hypothesi* it is in virtue of assigning a structural description that you have the conscious musical experience you do—that you hear or, as we often say, *feel* the music as you do. For example, it's in virtue of assigning such an analysis that you feel the tonic as being the most stable pitch in a scale, or an accent as being relatively strong in its metrical context, or a harmonic progression as being "tense" or "relaxed." As Lerdahl and Jackendoff will put it, having the right sort of musical structure in your head is what *understanding* the music consists in:[20]

> [T]he understanding of a piece of music by the idealized listener consists in his finding the maximally coherent structural description or descriptions which can be associated with the piece's sequence of pitch-time events (1977, 118).[21]

The M-grammar consists of four sets of (largely recursive) analytical rules whose closest linguistic relatives are the syntactic phrase structure rules outlined above. (Since the few musical transformation rules play a minimal role in the theory, we shall not examine them here.) Very roughly, *metrical* and *grouping* rules analyze rhythmic structure, while higher-level *time-span* and *prolongational* rules analyze certain interactions between rhythm and pitch.[22] A brief look at a musical structural description will help to clarify things. In figure 2.2, [23] dots immediately below the score, assigned by the metrical rules, indicate relative beat strength, while brackets assigned by the grouping rules segment the piece into motives, phrases, and sections. The more abstract tree structure or time-span reduction shown above the score is inferred from the

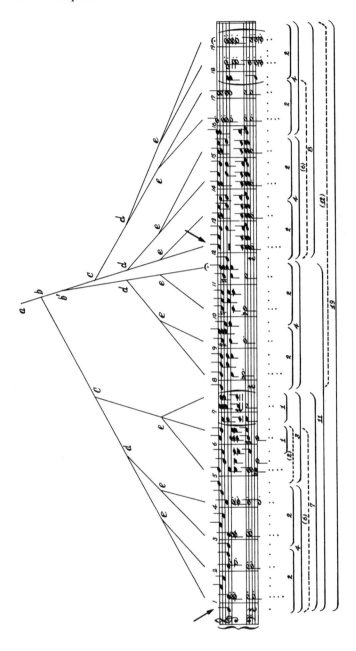

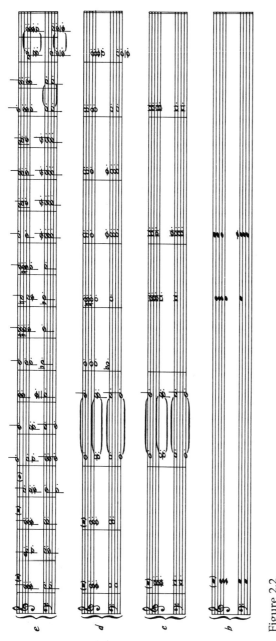

Figure 2.2
Metrical, grouping, and time-span analyses of Schubert, "Morgengruss" (Lerdahl and Jackendoff 1983, 265).

metrical and grouping analyses and specifies a hierarchy of structural importance (a "reduction") among all the pitch-time events in the piece. The higher the level attained by a given branch in the time-span analysis, the greater the structural importance of the musical event to which the branch attaches; thus events (e.g., the downbeat of bar 12, at arrow) whose branches reach level *a* are (heard or "felt" as being) more important than events (e.g., the downbeat of bar 1, at arrow) whose branches reach level *b*, those that reach *b* more important than those that reach *c*, and so forth. Finally, a fourth type of analysis, the prolongational reduction (figure 2.3), is inferred from the time-span reduction. This most abstract representation specifies the relative structural importance of pitch-time events "in terms of continuity and progression, the movement toward tension or relaxation, and the degree of closure or nonclosure" (1983, 123). For example, the fact that the tonic (I) harmony of bar 1 branches left with an open circle from the tonic (I) harmony of bar 12 (see arrows) means that the former is felt as a *strong prolongation* or *anticipation* of the latter.

Although the operations of the four sets of rules are clearly distinguishable, none of the four components functions in isolation from the other three. Indeed, inter-component feedback is common, as evinced for example in Grouping Preference Rule 7:

> Prefer a grouping structure that results in more stable time-span and/or prolongational reductions (52)

and Time-span Reduction Preference Rule 5:

> In choosing the head of a time-span T, prefer a choice that results in a more stable choice of metrical structure (165).

For the discussion that follows, it will be important to understand that the musical representations can be ordered with respect to abstractness ("distance" or "depth" from transducer outputs) along at least two dimensions. Along one dimension, which I shall call the "low/ high" dimension, meter and grouping are on a par as the *lowest* (hence least abstract) levels of analysis, followed by time-span structure and then prolongational structure at progressively *higher* (more abstract) levels. These distinctions in respect of "height" reflect the fact that time-span structure is inferred from the metrical and grouping segmentations, and prolongational structure in turn from the time-span reduc-

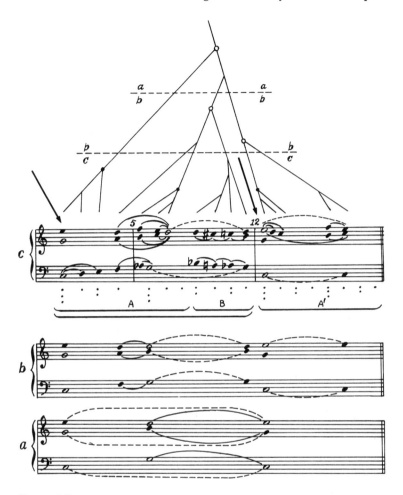

Figure 2.3
Prolongational analysis of Schubert, "Morgengruss" (Lerdahl and
Jackendoff 1983, 267.)

tion (allowing, again, for lots of inter-component feedback). Along a second dimension, the "local/global" dimension, *local* (hence least abstract) levels are distinguished from *global* (hence most abstract) levels *within* the analysis computed by each of the four sets of rules. The local/global distinction reflects the fact that events registering at relatively deeper levels in a given type of analysis are structurally important over relatively larger regions of the piece; intuitively speaking, the deeper the level at which a given event registers, the more *global* its structural importance. In the time-span reduction shown above, for example, events registering at level *c* are structurally important over larger regions of the piece than are events registering at levels *d* and *e*.[24] The idea then is that, on the low/high dimension, prolongational structure is more abstract than time-span structure, and the latter in turn more abstract than metrical and grouping structure; while on the local/global dimension, global levels are more abstract than local levels *within* each of the four types of analysis. Of course, this is not yet to say anything about the order of real-time processing; we come to that shortly.

For the most part we need not trouble over the details of the M-grammatical rules. However, a certain feature of the time-span and prolongational components that will figure centrally in our project here, and a brief remark about that is in order. As we have just heard, these two sets of rules generate hierarchies of structural importance among the pitches of a piece in light of the metrical and grouping segmentations. In order to do this, they must "have access" to general criteria of pitch importance or stability. Lerdahl and Jackendoff explain:

> [We] take as given the classical Western tonal pitch system—the major-minor scale system, the traditional classifications of consonance and dissonance, the triadic harmonic system with its roots and inversions, the circle-of-fifths system, and the principles of good voice leading. Though all of these principles could and should be formalized . . . [n]othing will be lost if we conveniently consider them to be an input to the theory of reductions. . . . What is needed, in addition, is a scale of stability among pitch configurations, derived from the raw material of the given tonal system. Broadly, the relative stability of a pitch-event can be thought of in terms of its relative consonance or dissonance (1977, 117).[25]

The thought is that in the time-span and prolongational analyses, information about the rhythmic location and importance of pitch-time events is brought into register with long-term mental representations or *schemas* of the pitch relationships that define our Western tonal system. The results of this interplay of rhythmic and pitch information are hierarchical specifications of the overall relative structural importance of events in the piece. Lerdahl and Jackendoff do not elucidate further the nature of these schematic structures, but we shall have occasion to learn more about them as our story unfolds.

The structural description is so called because it represents the signal as instantiating the basic structural elements of the music—namely its pitches and rhythms—as well as the more abstract structural features inferred therefrom.[26] In calling these the *structural* features, I mean *inter alia* that they constitute a system of elements whose tokens are (1) discrete, (2) type-identifiable by some finite mechanical procedure, and (3) combinable in certain rule-governed ways. (Philosophers might say that such a system has a syntax, but I shall refrain from using that term here so as to avoid any confusion with its special sense in linguistic theory.) The structural description does not, at least not explicitly, capture what I shall call the *nonstructural* features of the music. Dynamics (loudness levels), tempi (perceived speeds), and timbres (tone "colors") come immediately to mind, but as we shall soon see, even pitch and rhythm, those paradigmatically structural elements, have their nonstructural aspects as well. For the time being I shall characterize the nonstructural features, unhelpfully, as those audible features of the music that fail to satisfy the trio of conditions just cited; but we shall learn a lot more about them in chapters 4 and 5.

Although the nonstructural features of the music are not explicitly represented in the structural description, they are often influential in its formation. As Lerdahl and Jackendoff acknowledge, "[t]hese dimensions play an important role in the theory in that they make crucial contributions to the principles that establish the hierarchical structure for a piece. The theory thus takes into account the influence of [nonstructural] dimensions, even though it does not formalize them" (1983, 9). Just for example, the pattern of strong and weak beats assigned by the metrical rules may depend significantly on sudden changes in the loudness of pitch-time events, while the placement of phrase boundaries by the grouping rules may be sensitive to variations in speed.

2.3 The Fodor Connection

The foregoing presentation of the M-grammatical rules was of course no more than a peek at the Lerdahl-Jackendoff theory. Nevertheless, it should suffice to bring out the kinship between the M-grammar and Fodor's input systems: music perception or understanding is said to proceed via the inference of a series of increasingly abstract mental representations of an acoustic stimulus.[27] Not surprisingly, the most perspicuous analogy extends to Fodor's treatment of language processing; as we have heard:

> [A]ccording to all standard theories, the computations that input systems perform typically proceed via the assignment of a number of intermediate analyses of the proximal stimulation. Sentence comprehension, for example, involves not only acoustic encoding but also the recovery of phonetic and lexical content and syntactic form (56)....Understanding a token sentence presumably involves assigning it a structural description...and that is precisely the sort of function we would expect an input system to perform (44).

Fodor envisions the linguistic input system as equipped with Chomsky-style phonetic, lexical, syntactic, and perhaps also logical rules. Inevitably, theorists of language disagree as to the precise architecture of the L-grammar and the order in which its various rules are applied; but however the details are worked out, the fundamental insight is that linguistic understanding is the yield of a series of increasingly abstract representations of an acoustic stimulus, a substantial number of which are generated according to grammatical rules. Lerdahl and Jackendoff paint an analogous picture of music perception, hypothesizing that "comprehension involves not only acoustic encoding but also the recovery of" metrical, grouping, time-span, and prolongational structure as prescribed by grammatical rules.

With this theoretical scaffolding in place, let me suggest how the musical story might go. As I observed earlier, we can assume that perception originates with the transduction of acoustic properties of the sound signal. Representations of the psychoacoustic correlates to those transduced properties (pitch for frequency, loudness for intensity, and so forth) are presumably then inferred in parallel from the transducer outputs. Whether temporal features are transduced is not clear, but one way or another the durations of events will need to be recovered at a relatively shallow level. Once you have pitch and duration you have pitch-time events, the basic psychological building blocks of tonal music.[28] And once you have pitch-time events, the machinery of the M-grammar can be engaged; in other words, a structural description can be computed. (Actually, the preceding two sentences are misleading, for reasons that come to light in chapter 4; but they will do for now.) The operations of the grammatical rules are unconscious, but of course the *results* of those operations ultimately gain entry into conscious awareness: the whole point of the M-grammar is to differentiate pitch-time events in a way that affords the conscious musical experience we know and love—the characteristic feelings of beat strength, tonal center, stability, tension, relaxation, and so forth. The hypothesis is that music sounds the way it does, that we have the musical experiences or feelings we do, *in virtue of* generating these underlying structural representations.

2.4 Tying Up the Loose Ends

I have been simplifying things quite a bit in order to emphasize just how comfortably the Lerdahl-Jackendoff model meshes with Fodor's account of inferential perceptual systems. Such interdisciplinary bedfellows are rarely so neat, and a little tidying up is in order.

In the first place, as it stands, the M-grammar is a formal competence model; that is to say, the structural description it assigns to the music models only the idealized final state of the experienced listener's understanding of a musical work (Lerdahl and Jackendoff 1983, 4). In particular, the grammatical theory says nothing (or, anyway, very little) about the manner in which a structural description is assigned to a musical stimulus as the latter unfolds "in real time." Fodor, on the other hand, means to be offering something much more like a real-time processing model of perception. Thus although I have made a few cursory remarks about the probable character of peripheral musical processes (viz. transduction and the recovery of psychoacoustic correlates), the desired affiliation with Fodor's theory demands a clearer picture of the real-time processing of *grammatical* levels of representation. Happily, Jackendoff (1987) has proposed a processing model that shares its output, to a significant extent, with the musical competence model.[29]

Jackendoff reasons that, since the structure assigned to a given event in the music depends on the structure assigned to surrounding events, it is plausible to suppose that at any point in its analysis of a piece, the music processor is both "recalling" what went before and "guessing" what comes next. Accordingly, he proposes that real-time ("on-line") music perception consists in projecting, as each new pitch-time event is heard, a multiplicity of possible structural analyses of events heard so far—analyses complying with a variety of possible subsequent developments. Sometimes the processor will be able to select from among the various projected alternatives a single most "salient" analysis, sometimes not; if not, the resulting musical experience is likely to be one of uncertainty or instability. In some instances, information from incoming events will force the processor to revise its previous analysis, bringing about a "retrospective reanalysis" (1987, 243); in such a case the listener may experience a kind of auditory Gestalt shift, resulting in a feeling of surprise. Be the details as they may, as the music progresses, more and more possible analyses are eliminated in light of new developments until, at the end, a unique best analysis remains.

Actually, the "uniqueness" issue is somewhat obscure. Jackendoff's view seems to be that, typically, by the end of any given hearing of a piece, one's music processor has selected a unique best ("most preferred" or "maximally coherent") structural description from among the various alternatives it has projected along the way. And that much seems entirely plausible. In addition, however, the nature of our musical experience suggests that, in another hearing by the same listener—*a fortiori* in a hearing by a different listener—a different description may be selected as the maximally coherent one from among a different set of alternatives (or, for that matter, from among the same set of alternatives). It seems plausible to suppose that the music you have been listening to recently and the kind of training you have had, among other things, will often influence your expectations as to what a piece is going to do next; and what you expect it to do next will inevitably influence the possible structures you project for events heard so far. Furthermore, it seems likely that the structure you assign in any given hearing will be influenced by the character of the performance heard; for example, the performer's manipulation of fine details ("nuances") of timing, loudness, and articulation *inter alia* may significantly affect your selection of phrase boundaries and various prolongational relationships (cf., e.g., Lerdahl and Jackendoff 1983, 63–64 and Palmer 1988). My thought, then, is that insofar as the course of real-time processing is influenced by these sorts of factors, we can expect that the structural description selected for a given work by a given listener—*a fortiori* the descriptions selected by different listeners—will vary from one hearing to another. (I shall return to the variability of real-time perception in §2.5.)

The variabilities notwithstanding, this real-time processing model poses no special problems for our inferential account of music perception. Assigning a structural description still consists in inferring metrical and grouping, time-span, and prolongational structures (in roughly that order), with the sorts of feedback exchanges mentioned earlier; it's just that in real-time processing these inferences are bootstrapped "from left to right," as it were, over time. We can think of the projected structural descriptions as hypotheses about how the piece is to be heard (i.e., what its maximally coherent structural description is), and the eventual selection of one among these as the confirmation of that hypothesis. The final output of music processing—that is, the conscious "percept"—is presumably a maximally coherent prolongational reduction supplemented with representations of nonstructural features like loudness, timbre, articulation, and speed. Call this output the 'supplemented prolongational reduction'.[30]

A final clarification. Thus far I have spoken more or less indifferently of stimuli, tones, sounds, signals, pieces, works, performances, and music. In light of the preceding discussion, we can now institute a more careful taxonomy. (Keep in mind, however, that what follows is intended only to clarify my usage of certain terms; I do not mean to be defining or supplying identity conditions here, and what I say below is incomplete and courts circularity in places.) Henceforth, 'stimulus', 'tone', 'sound', and 'signal' will refer to an acoustic object as such; 'piece' and 'work' will refer to a certain sort of abstract object, roughly a class of structures including at least some of the structures recovered in at least some of the maximally coherent structural descriptions of the sequence of pitch-time events prescribed by a given score; and 'performance of a musical work' will refer to an acoustic object as produced "in compliance with" the instructions in the relevant score.[31] I shall continue to use the term 'music' in a loose way to refer to both works and their performances; where the distinction is important, I shall say explicitly what I have in mind.

In stipulating these usages I make a number of assumptions. Perhaps most important, I assume (with Lerdahl and Jackendoff among others) that the M-grammatical rules specify at least part of the structure constitutive of a musical work. But of course the point is debatable: for instance, who's to say the correct analysis of the music isn't prescribed by a different set of purely compositional principles? The composer of a tonal work (*a fortiori* of an atonal one) may follow compositional rules that are not psychologically real and hence bear no significant relationship to the rules that govern listening.[32] (Maybe the compositional rules are too complicated, or would demand too much storage capacity, or do not take sufficient account of structural symmetries, etc.) In that case, since an appeal to the compositional rules would likely provide the most coherent and compelling analysis of the music, one might reasonably insist that *they,* and not the M-grammatical rules, specify the structure of the work; at the very least, some argument would be required to show otherwise. For the most part I shall skirt this issue here, though it will obviously want attention in a full dress theory of musical understanding. At present I shall simply assume that the structures assigned by the (correct) M-grammar include at least *some* of the structures belonging to the work in question. Apart from such an assumption it is hard to see how experienced listeners could acquire knowledge or understanding of a piece just by hearing it; and *surely* tonal music is the sort of thing that can be known in the hearing.

With this cognitivist foundation in place, we are positioned to introduce the first two kinds of ineffable musical knowledge cited at the beginning. A brief discussion of the first concludes this chapter; a rather more lengthy discussion of the second is the subject of chapter 3. What will prove central in the discussion that follows are a pair of now familiar hypotheses: first, that music perception consists in the inference of a series of increasingly abstract mental representations of an acoustic signal, as detailed above; and second, that those representations reflect a distinction between structural and nonstructural features of the music.

2.5 A First Candidate for Ineffable Musical Knowledge

In an obvious and not very interesting sense, the content of any musical structural description is exhaustively "effable": every rule and formalism employed in the M-grammatical theory—including metrical dots, grouping brackets, tree structures, and the various notations in the musical score—can be rendered in explicit verbal form. (For example, the structural description in figure 2.2 specifies a passage in 3/4 time, in the key of C major, opening with a G-natural quarter-note upbeat to a C major chord on the downbeat of the first bar; the upbeat is the initial event in a group extending through the second beat of the second bar, etc.) But of course that much by itself tells us nothing about the character of real-time musical experience, the subject of our reflections here. What is significant for our purposes is the fact that, in principle, a suitably trained listener can report the grammatical structure he consciously *hears* or *feels* in the music: he can tell us that he consciously feels the tonic, or the downbeat, or a weak prolongation, or a plagal cadence.[33] I say he can do this *in principle*. Typically, a trained listener will have no difficulty reporting the structures assigned in relatively local levels of his structural descriptions; for all intents and purposes, he will be able to report the pitches, rhythms, and time signature of a heard piece (i.e., he'll be able to "recover the score"), along with some local levels of grouping, time-span, and prolongational structure *inter alia*. (Just how he does this is a topic we shall take up in chapter 4.) Furthermore, insofar as the more global levels of structure are no different *in kind* from the local ones, it seems fair to say that in principle the trained listener can report the entire (conscious) content of his structural description of the music. However—and here is the important point for a theory of ineffability—the vicissitudes of real-time perception are likely to pose certain obstacles to full verbal disclosure, especially of some of the more global levels of analysis. Or so I am going to suggest.

In my experience, episodes of the following sort are common. Having easily reported the pitches, rhythms, and time signature of a heard piece, along perhaps with some of its local grouping, time-span, and prolongational structures, a listener (perhaps even a highly expert one) finds himself at a loss: "I am feeling that E-natural in a certain distinctive way, but I can't say just how. I know it's the leading tone, and that it's preparing the return to the tonic, and I know it's a weak prolongation of the E-natural in the previous bar . . . but somehow I feel there is more going on." Or a performer feels himself compelled to play a certain passage in a certain way (e.g., to slow down, or to get louder, or to increase the vibrato speed)—consciously feels, knows, that it must be played thus, and yet cannot say why. (Again, he can tell us what the pitches, rhythms, and time signatures are.) Such cases, it seems to me, are plausibly described as instances of ineffable musical *knowledge:* we (consciously) know more than we can say. What I want to suggest is that unconscious structural representations—in particular, relatively global levels of representation—are "making themselves felt" in our conscious experience, yet their contents elude our verbal grasp: we cannot say which structures are represented. I shall call this ineffability the *structural* ineffability, signifying that it attaches to our conscious knowledge of musical structure. Sometimes the structural ineffability dissolves, or anyway seems to dissolve, with explicit music-theoretic analysis: one applies pencil to score and discovers an element of the musical architecture that seems, intuitively, to account for the character of the experience—for instance, for the way that E-natural sounded: it was also a prolongation of an E-natural eight bars earlier, and that's why it sounded the way it did. In many instances, however, the ineffability persists, shrouding the music in its characteristic mystery.

Why might such a structural ineffability arise? Here is a speculation (and *just* a speculation).

I remarked above that we are both inter- and intrasubjectively pretty consistent in our reports of (at least some) local levels of musical structure; for all practical purposes, everyone reports the same pitches, rhythms, time-signatures, and various other local features, in every hearing of a given work. On the other hand, insofar as we *are* able to report the more global or large-scale musical structures we hear, significant variation is apparent. It can hardly be incidental that trained listeners argue about where the phrase boundaries are in a piece (phrases are relatively large-scale grouping structures), and not about what its pitches and rhythms are, for example. Moreover, as we saw earlier, reflection on the character of our musical experience, plus a good deal of data from recent psychological studies, suggests that one and the same listener may assign different phrasings to a given work in different hearings of it. Presumably a similar variability attends our perception of other large-scale structures. In general, then, it appears that *ceteris paribus* we have greater difficulty reporting global structures than local ones, and the reports we do make of global structures are less consistent, both within and across subjects, than our reports of local structures.[34] That is what I shall suppose, anyway, for purposes of my present speculation.

Now on the cognitivist view we endorse, the best explanation for the consistency in our reports of local structures is a corresponding consistency in our underlying mental representations; and similarly, *mutatis mutandis*, for the disparities in our reports of more global structures. One could (though I won't here) speculate at length as to the reasons for this local/global difference; but whatever the reasons for the apparently greater leeway in our analyses at global levels, it seems plausible to suppose that these latter are susceptible to the variable influences of a number of factors. First of all, the complexity, sophistication, and sheer number of maximally coherent structural descriptions a listener can infer are likely to vary with his genetic endowment, type of training, and listening history, along with any structural cues supplied by the nuances of a given performance. Generally speaking, the trained listener is presumably equipped to recover all manner of structural relations lost on his untutored counterpart. But furthermore, the connoisseur of Mozart, steeped in the architectonic of the Classical period, may recover sectional symmetries in the *Jupiter* that go unnoticed by the lover of Wagner. Glenn Gould and Rosalynn Tureck slow down at different places in the *Goldberg Variations;* hence one who hears Gould's performance may locate the phrase boundaries rather differently than one who hears Tureck's. (All things being equal, players tend to slow down at phrase boundaries; see, e.g., Palmer 1989, 1992.) A genius like Gunther Schuller may hear the penultimate chord of a movement as prolonging a chord at the beginning, whereas I, who cannot "hold" such large-scale relationships in my head, hear nothing. (Again, everyone agrees on the pitches and rhythms.) Indeed, this intersubjective variability in our assignments of global structures may account for the need to communicate our musical knowledge: we want others to hear what we hear, know what we know. Cavell's words speak eloquently to our concerns here:

It is not merely that I want to tell you how it is with me, how I
feel. . . . It's rather that I want to tell you something I've seen, or
heard, or realized, or come to understand, for the reasons for which
such things are communicated (because it is news about a world
we share, or could. . . . It matters that others know what I [hear],
in a way it does not matter whether they know my tastes. . . . Art
is often praised because it brings men together. But it also separates
them (1967, 78–80).

In addition, as I remarked above, training and listening history, as well
as the recovery of performers' "interpretative" cues, may cause variations at global levels of analysis even over repeated hearings by a single
subject. For instance, if you listen to other music during the interim
between hearings of a given work, or if you listen to different performances of the same work, the phrasings you assign may differ as a
result; and a Ravel waltz heard as a sequence of scalar permutations
may sustain global prolongational relationships quite different from
those sustained in its hearing as a sequence of chord functions. (Perhaps
it is for such reasons that we enjoy repeated hearings of the same work—
nay, the same performance.)

My thought then is this. With sufficient explicit knowledge of the
M-grammatical rules and enough practice at matching the grammatical
geography with the introspective—that is, with enough knowledge of
what kinds of musical structures give rise to what kinds of conscious
experience—the listener will get very good at reporting the contents
of his structural descriptions of the music. Or, rather, he will get very
good at reporting the contents of their local levels, which are, as I have
observed, more or less consistent across hearings. At more global levels,
however, it seems likely that the (hypothesized) variability of structures
assigned would greatly hamper any effort to learn, and hence to report,
which kinds of structure are consciously "known" in which kinds of
experience or feeling. Crudely: if you assigned the same global structures to a piece every time you heard it (*a fortiori* if *everyone* assigned
those same structures on every hearing), then there might be some
chance of learning to report what those structures are; but you don't,
and so there isn't. At any given time, the underlying structural description will "make itself felt" in the current phenomenology, to be sure;
that is the sense, if any, in which you consciously know its content. But

the likelihood seems vanishingly small that you will be able to *say*, exhaustively anyway, what that content is. To this extent, I suggest, you have conscious but ineffable knowledge of the music: you know something you cannot put into words.

I do not deny, of course, that you may be able to enunciate the "idealized" structural analysis that would be assigned by the grammatical *competence* model. But that analysis is based primarily on the information specified in the score and so will fail to take into account many of the variables that appear to influence on-line perception. Intuitively speaking, the competence model will not tell you which global structures you actually assign in any particular real-time hearing of a piece (though for obvious reasons it will usually get the local structures right). The competence model won't take into account, for example, the fact that you hear a certain note in the Stravinsky *Serenade in A* as increasing rather than (as the competence model might have it) decreasing in tension because you are expecting a modulation of the kind that occurs in the twelfth bar of a Chopin ballade you've been practicing all week. It is the entrance of the latter sort of influence that makes reporting your real-time structural analyses so difficult.[35]

2.6 Looking Ahead

The foregoing proposal is, of course, highly speculative, frequently anecdotal, and even if true, surely not complete. Nevertheless, I think it looks in the right place for an account of at least one variety of ineffable musical knowledge; and in any case it provides an idea of the *kind* of explanation our cognitivist approach has to offer.

Even so, the structural ineffability may seem a toothless sort. As I observed above, our on-line knowledge of musical structure is effable in principle: the structures that are known ineffably are no different *in kind* from the structures we can report. Surely, in serenading our "wealth of wordless knowledge," theorists like Cavell and Langer and Dewey had something meatier in mind. In the next chapter we shall uncover a second brand of musical ineffability—one which, though closely tied to the structural kind, comes somewhat closer to hitting the traditional mark.[36]

Chapter 3
Does Music Mean What It Cannot Say?

Do we not, in truth, ask the impossible of music when we expect it to express feelings?

Igor Stravinsky 1942, 77

3.1 A Second Candidate for Ineffable Knowledge

What is it to know a piece of music? Our answer, provisionally, is that knowing a piece consists at least partly in having a certain kind of sensory-perceptual representation in your head—specifically, a structural description as detailed by Lerdahl and Jackendoff.[1] To be conscious of that knowledge is to be conscious of the content of that representation. Here, conscious knowledge takes the form of certain peculiarly musical feelings: we experience the feeling of rhythmic stress that comes with hearing (representing) an acoustic event as the downbeat, the feeling of stability that comes with hearing a given tone as the tonic, the feelings of tension and resolution that come with hearing a series of events as a harmonic progression, and so on. (For clarity's sake I shall call these feelings, simply, the 'musical feelings'; we shall hear a good deal more about them as we go along.) Waxing expansive, one might say that in the musical realm, conscious knowledge, understanding, intuition, sense-perception, experience, and feeling come together. It is often claimed that aesthetic experience is characterized by a convergence of mental "activities" elsewhere held apart: in the artistic realm, understanding *is* perceiving, knowing *is* feeling.

Cavell's words echo clearly here: works of (musical) art are "only *known by feeling.*" One gloss might be: knowledge of a musical work is sensory-perceptual or "experiential" or "felt" knowledge; mere "propositional" or "descriptive" knowledge won't do.[2] Granted, to *know that* a piece is in A major, or *that* it opens with an ascending perfect fourth, or *that* it is in sonata form, is to know something about the piece, to have some knowledge of it. But to *know the piece*, in the preeminent sense of that locution, is to know *how it sounds* or, as we sometimes say, *how it feels*. Cavell:

> [T]he first fact about art [is] that it must be felt, not merely known— or, as I would rather put it, that it must be known for oneself. It is a statement of the fact of life—the metaphysical fact, one could say—that apart from one's experience of [a piece of music] there is nothing to *be* known about it (1967, 114).

Such ways of talking are redolent with intimations of ineffable knowledge. But where exactly does the ineffability lie?

I have suggested that our conscious knowledge of the music we hear is structurally effable in principle (cf. §§2.5-2.6). The other side of the coin, of course, is that in principle a trained listener can *acquire* conscious knowledge of the structure of a work simply by being told, or reading, what that structure is. And I do not mean that he thereby acquires (mere) *descriptive* knowledge of it; on the contrary, such a listener comes to know how the music sounds or feels, in just the way you know how this sentence sounds without having to hear it uttered, or how a red object looks without having to lay eyes on it. To operationalize the point, the trained listener acquires *recognitional* sensory-perceptual knowledge of musical structures from a verbal report thereof; that is to say, he can recognize their instantiations (performances) by ear. Paul Churchland illustrates the point in this way:

> [I]f a set of notes is specified verbally, a trained pianist or guitarist can identify the chord and recall its sound in auditory imagination. Moreover, a really skilled individual can construct, in auditory imagination, the sound of a chord he may never have heard before, and certainly does not remember. Specify for him a relatively unusual one—an F#9th-add13th for example—and let him brood for a bit. Then play for him three or four chords, one of which is the target, and see whether he can pick it out as the sound that meets the description. Skilled musicians can do this (1985, 26).

I do not mean to contend that in such a case one experiences the musical feelings, "in imagination" as it were, in the same robust way one experiences them in real-time perception; no doubt there are significant disparities between imagination and perception. I don't propose to worry about those here, however, since it seems to me obvious that the recognitional knowledge Churchland describes is conscious in a perfectly straightforward sense of the term. One might say that, at a minimum, such knowledge is consciously mobilized in the (conscious) activity of recognizing a musical structure by ear.

As with the trained listener's report of his knowledge of musical structure, his success in the "knowledge acquisition" task is likely to be greatest (*ceteris paribus*) in respect of relatively local levels of structure, deteriorating as the structures in question become more global and/or complex (as with chords containing many pitches).[3] But again, the global structures are no different *in kind* from the local ones; hence we are entitled to say that, in principle, the trained listener can acquire conscious recognitional knowledge of musical structures from a report thereof. In the next chapter I shall explain in some detail how he does this; for now, all we need to know is that he *can* do it.

Such impressive recognitional abilities notwithstanding, what must be appreciated is that a listener acquires musical knowledge from verbal reports and score readings only insofar as they cause in him the formation of the right sorts of *sensory-perceptual* representations. And he can form the right sorts of sensory-perceptual representations only if he has had the right sorts of (auditory) *experiences* at some time or other. In order to acquire musical knowledge "by description," a listener has already got to know—in the sense of being able to recognize by ear—how the twelve chromatic intervals sound and how the rhythmic values and stress patterns that define metrical structure sound. And all the talk in the world won't get him that.[4]

Let me be quite clear. I am precisely *not* suggesting that actual sense-perception of (performances of) a particular work is necessary for knowledge of it. Walter Gieseking is famously said to have learned the Pfitzner piano concerto "from the score" while journeying by train to Berlin for the concert, victim of a last-minute program change; did he not thereby come to know the piece?[5] Beethoven was deaf by the time he wrote the ninth symphony and so never heard a performance of it; didn't he know the work even so? Good musicians perform feats of this kind, albeit less prodigious ones, all the time. The point is, once the requisite sensory-perceptual "schemas" are ensconced in long-term memory, the trained listener can come to know a piece *by description*— by being told its pitches and rhythms, or by reading the score, or, like Beethoven, by "writing" the score in his mind. What remains true, however, is that such knowledge acquisition presupposes his having had certain sorts of sensory-perceptual experiences at some time or other. Musical knowledge—at least the sort of knowledge we standardly mean to ascribe when we say of someone that he "knows the music"— is *sensory-perceptual* or *experiential* or *felt* knowledge; and as such, it cannot be communicated by language *ab initio*. A person deaf from birth cannot know a piece of music. In this second respect, then, musical knowledge is ineffable knowledge.

3.2 Does Music Mean?

We seem to have put our finger on a second species of musical ineffability, which for want of a better name I shall call the *feeling ineffability*. Although stronger than the structural kind—our conscious structural knowledge would be "feeling ineffable" even if we could *in fact* report all of the contents of our structural descriptions—this second brand of wordless knowledge too may seem implausibly prosaic. After all, many features of our everyday world are known "only by feeling": the green shade of the apples on my kitchen counter, the volume of my telephone bell, the taste of last night's chicken curry, are similarly ineffable— knowledge of them is sensory-perceptual or felt knowledge—yet it ignites no expressive yearnings, inspires no soliloquies from the likes of Cavell and Langer. What is so special about musical objects that our ineffable knowledge of them commands our attention and demands to be named?

"The first fact of works of art," Cavell writes, "is that they are meant, meant to be understood" (1967, 123). It is of course a familiar idea that works of art are expressions of a sort—"utterances," Cavell calls them; and if (as seems likely) our paradigm of expression is linguistic, then that may help to explain why we are forever wanting to *say* what we hear, feel, *know*, in a piece of music. As Langer observes, "we are so deeply impressed with the paragon of symbolic form, namely language, that we naturally carry its characteristics over into our conceptions and expectations of any other mode" (1953, 28–29). Indeed our talk of *understanding* and *interpreting* the music only reinforces such a picture.

But of course none of that is special to music among the (non-linguistic) arts. What sets music apart, lending it a unique kinship to language, is its apparent possession of grammatical structure—or, more properly, the listener's apparent possession of (domain-specific) psychological rules for apprehending that structure. In linguistics, the unconscious structural description of a sentence is typically conceived as mapping a phonological representation into a semantic one; and whatever else it may be, the content of that semantic representation is, by its very nature, effable. After all, the whole point of the linguistic grammar is to enable communication *by language*. A plausible thought, then, is that the presence of grammatical structure in music, likewise recovered by rule-governed operations from acoustic stimuli, (mis)leads us to expect something similarly effable. Cavell says: "We follow the progress of a piece the way we follow what someone is saying" (1967, 85).[6] But of course what we "follow" a piece *to*, the results of grammatical processing, are the ineffable feelings that constitute our conscious musical knowledge or understanding. Perhaps it is the expectation of something like a linguistic semantics—something effable—that makes us notice the "feeling" ineffability in our musical knowledge, as opposed to our knowledge of the apples and the telephone bell, and even, perhaps, of a piece of sculpture, or an etching, or a ballet.

I said that music's grammatical structure may mislead us into semantic temptation. Music may be intended, but it isn't intentional: it isn't *about* anything. Except in certain contrived circumstances I shall discuss shortly, music does not refer or bear truth. Nevertheless, as the remarks of the preceding paragraph suggest, it may be appropriate to envision the musical feelings as an ineffable *analogue* to a semantics—a "quasi-semantics," as I shall call it. ('Pseudosemantics' rolls more smoothly off the tongue, but I don't want the negative connotations.) So much has been written on the subject of musical meaning, and so much of it is, in my view, wrongheaded, that it will be worth a somewhat lengthy digression to motivate the picture I have in mind. That will be my project for the remainder of this chapter.

Of course, the formulation and evaluation of any theory of musical meaning will ultimately require answers to a daunting collection of questions. For instance, is musical meaning or quasi-meaning, if such there be, more like the meaning of a sentence or like the meaning of a snapshot, or of a grin, or of an electron trace, or of life? Answering this question will in turn require that we explicate each of these various brands of meaning, and the challenges of that exercise are well known. Just for starters, does a linguistic expression get its meaning from its truth conditions, or from the abstract sense or proposition it expresses, or from the ways we use it, or from the mental state whose content it conveys, or from something else altogether? Tracing a path through this thicket is only made the more difficult by the ambiguity of the term 'meaning' as between, roughly, *content* and *value:* compare ' "Bachelor" means "unmarried man" with 'Your support means a lot to me'.[7]

In the face of these perplexities, my present goals are modest. They are two: first, to assemble some of the considerations favoring a quasi-semantics of musical feelings; and second, to show why such a view is preferable to at least some other theories of musical meaning that have been proposed.

3.3 *Setting the Stage*

A recurrent theme in the history of musical scholarship has it that music has meaning, or symbolic content, or semantics, or, at the very least, something you would want to call "significance." Not surprisingly, it is a theme with many variations: Schopenhauer (1958) will contend that music expresses the inner nature of the metaphysical will, Goodman (1968) that it metaphorically exemplifies properties like fragility and heroism,[8] Kuhns that it represents itself: "Tones in music represent other tones. A modulation from major to minor refers as it moves, and establishes referring relationships as it sounds" (1978, 122). The most prevalent strain by far, however, has it that music somehow symbolizes human *emotions.* Langer (1942, 1953) will claim that music symbolizes the dynamic forms of human feeling, Collingwood (1938) that it expresses an emotion in the mind of the composer, Dowling and Harwood that it "*represents* emotions in a way that can be recognized by listeners" (1986, 203). Roger Scruton has recently written that

[t]o understand musical meaning . . . is to understand how the cultivated ear can discern, in what it hears, the occasions for sympathy. I do not know *how* this happens; but *that* it happens is one of the given facts of musical culture. . . . Let us consider an example. In the slow movement of Schubert's G Major Quartet, D.887, there is a tremolando passage of the kind that you would describe as foreboding. Suddenly there shoots up from the murmuring sea of anxiety a single terrified gesture, a gesture of utter hopelessness and horror. . . . No one can listen to this passage without instantly sensing the object of this terror—without knowing, in some way, that death itself has risen on that unseen horizon. . . . In such instances we are being led by the ears towards a knowledge of the human heart (1987, 174–5).

Be the theoretical variations as they may, most contemporary scholars agree that whatever exactly musical meaning consists in, it bears little resemblance to meaning in the natural language. Peter Kivy, for one, contends that although music may be *expressive of*, say, tranquility or melancholia, it does not mean, in the way language means, anything at all:[9]

[U]nlike random noise or even ordered, periodic sound, music is quasi-syntactical; and where we have something like syntax, of course, we have one of the necessary properties of language. That is why music so often gives the strong impression of being meaningful. . . . [But] although musical meaning may exist as a theory, it does not exist as a reality of listening. . . . [I]t seems wonderful to me, and mysterious, that people sit for protracted periods of time doing nothing but listening to meaningless—yes, meaningless—strings of sounds (1990, 8–9, 12).

Indeed Lerdahl and Jackendoff themselves, champions of a linguistic approach to music, are similarly negative:

Many previous applications of linguistic methodology to music have foundered because they attempt a literal translation of some aspect of linguistic theory into musical terms—for instance, by looking for [a] musical . . . semantics. . . . [But this] is an old and largely futile game. . . . [W]hatever music may "mean," it is in no sense comparable to linguistic meaning (1983, 5-6).

I suspect that much of the skepticism about a musical/language parallel in the semantic arena results from a failure to recognize the variety of places at which such a parallel might gain its footing. In what follows I shall argue that our musical feelings are in certain respects precisely comparable to linguistic meanings; while I am sympathetic to the separatist line of Lerdahl and Jackendoff, I think it is overstated. Then I'll try to show that, whatever role the emotions may play in our musical understanding, it is not the one traditionally reserved for them. There is doubtless an intimate tie between our musical and affective lives, but the tie is not, in the sense envisioned, a *meaningful* one.

A final policy statement. It has been, and absent an explicit disclaimer on my part will continue to be, objected that a musical (quasi-)semantics of the kind I advance below is too restrictive. Just for example, Kathleen Higgins has recently charged that my cognitivist approach "validates structural characteristics as exclusively important for understanding music. It thus ignores other aspects of music that might be significant for our understanding" (1991, 213). In the interest of forestalling further such indictments, let me say explicitly that I make no pretense of offering "the compleat" theory of musical understanding or meaning. Various achievements may count as *understanding* the music; and a host of factors not treated here may be "significant for our understanding," ranging from considerations of historical context and population relativity to the moral and political character of the *avant-garde*.[10] There may be significant musical parallels to the tone of a linguistic utterance, or to its conversational implicatures, or to its performative force, to name just a few; I do not wish to detract from any of these. On the contrary, all I mean to show is that our cognitive-grammatical picture of musical understanding brings to light a musical feature that bears certain striking (and hitherto overlooked) similarities to a semantics for the natural language. Showing this will go a long way toward explaining the specialness of musical ineffability—that is, toward explaining why we notice and remark upon the (feeling) ineffability in our musical knowledge, as opposed to other familiar kinds of sensory-perceptual knowledge. I suggested that the apprehension of grammatical structure in music sets up the expectation of something analogous to a linguistic semantics. Now I am going to show that we do in fact *get* something analogous—but ineffable. This "surprises" us, violates our expectations, and so we notice it.

3.4 Meaning as Explanandum and Guide

I remarked above that music has no intentional content; it isn't about anything. Granted, if we set things up right we can *lend* the music a certain intentionality: to the listener armed with his glossary of Wagnerian leitmotifs, a given theme may assert, in some sense of 'assert', 'Here comes Siegfried'; to the listener informed of Stravinsky's intent, the descending Phrygian scale that opens *Orpheus* may refer, in some sense of 'refer', to the hero's ill-fated descent into Hades. Perhaps there are also various so-called pragmatic meanings borne by the performances (particular "utterances") of a work: imitating Isaac Stern's interpretation of the Ravel *Tzigane* during a performance of the piece in honor of Stern's birthday might, I suppose, be an example. At the very least, it makes sense to say that one can be *wrong* in such cases: if a leitmotif is Siegfried's and you take it for Brunhilde's, or if you take the performance for an imitation of Perlman rather than Stern, you are, in a pretty obvious sense, mistaken. And meaning, whatever else it may be, is the sort of thing you can be mistaken about. (I shall return to this point later on.)

Nevertheless, such instances of musical meaning are, as I shall put it, *dependent* on linguistic meanings.[11] That *Orpheus* opens with a descending scale and closes with the same scale in ascent is, of course, a stroke of genius; but those scales do not, *taken by themselves* as it were, mean anything about Orpheus at all. Crudely: somebody has got to *tell* you what they "mean." Similarly, you must consult your little glossary if you want to know which theme is which in a Wagner opera. Language, on the other hand, has what I shall call *independent* meaning. The point is obvious enough. Suppose you leave an arbitrarily selected, competent English speaker-hearer alone in a room with nothing but a passage of text in English (an article from the day's *New York Times*, say), and ask him to read it. Left entirely to his own devices, he'll understand it, he'll recover its meaning. Lacking various contextual cues, of course, he may miss some of its pragmatic import; but in a straightforward, indeed paradigmatic sense of 'understand', if he does not understand the article we shall want to say that *contra* hypothesis he is not competent in English. The thing about linguistic understanding, as Chomsky takes pains to point out, is that it's *creative:* competent speaker-hearers can (produce and) understand indefinitely many novel sentences of their language. (That, recall, is what the postulation of tacit grammatical knowledge is supposed to explain.) And then my point is that the variety of (musical) understanding in the Siegfried and Orpheus examples, by contrast, is *not* creative.

The recognition that music has no independent intentional content doubtless inspires much of the skepticism about a music/language parallel. However, that disparity should not blind us to other aspects of music and language that may yet provide the bridge we are looking for. As a start, I shall focus on two meta-theoretic roles played by a semantics for the natural language, and try to show that they support a robust musical analogy. First and foremost, understanding, the grasp of meaning, is the *explanandum* of the linguistic theory: specifically, the linguist postulates unconscious assignments of grammatical structure in order to explain how speaker-hearers understand the sentences of their language.[12] Second, and as a consequence, the linguist's postulation of grammatical structures is sometimes guided by an appeal to semantic considerations. Let me elaborate on this second, guiding role.

Consider the following passages (just a few among many, many examples) from two recent texts in linguistics—Geoffrey Horrocks's *Generative Grammar* (1987),[13] and Scott Soames and David Perlmutter's *Syntactic Argumentation and the Structure of English* (1979):

> [W]e cannot plausibly regard 'ignorance' as the nominalization of 'ignore' since, despite the formal relationship, their meanings are quite different. . . . Since it is assumed in the standard theory that deep structures provide all the syntactic and lexical information required for semantic interpretation, it is clear that transformations cannot be allowed to change meaning. . . . Hence we cannot derive 'ignorance' from 'ignore' by transformation (Horrocks, 57).

> [T]he idiomatic phrase ['keep tabs on'] may be seen as a particular instantiation of the complement structure of 'keep'; it has to be listed separately [in the lexicon] because unlike 'keep bikes in (the shed)', for example, it has a meaning which is not simply 'the sum of its parts' (Horrocks, 50).

Proper names are used to refer to specific individuals. As a result, when the head NP of a relative clause is a proper name, it picks out the subject of predication, leaving no role for a restrictive clause to play. Consequently, proper names cannot be heads of restrictive clauses (Soames and Perlmutter, 269).

Rejecting a phrase structure derivation of sentences like 'Harriet I spotted yesterday at the movies' and 'The Bahamas you said were warm in January',[14] Soames and Perlmutter explain that

> [e]ven if it were possible to generate [such] sentences in underlying structure, the grammar would need some device to capture the fact that the "extra NP" in initial position bears the semantic relations it would have if it were in the "gap" (239).

The details of these accounts, and their ultimate success as theories of grammatical structure, are unimportant in the present context. All I am concerned to show, and what the cited passages clearly attest, is that the theoretical postulation of linguistic grammatical (specifically, syntactic and lexical) structure is sometimes guided by an appeal to considerations of meaning: it is because 'ignore' and 'ignorance' are "quite different" in *meaning* that the theorist eschews a derivation of the latter from the former by transformation; it is the "noncompositionality" of the *meaning* of 'keep tabs on' that alerts the theorist to the need for a separate entry in the lexicon. In cases like these, the theorist's knowledge of meaning guides him in the assignment of grammatical structure. (Analogous examples could be mined from phonology as well—and, trivially, from semantics—but for purposes of a musical analogy, the syntactic and lexical cases are the most perspicuous.)

Perhaps it will be objected that, in principle, the theorist need be guided only by intuitions about syntactic and lexical structure, that the appeals to semantic factors are at best mere methodological shortcuts. And granted, were the theorist to have at hand a speaker-hearer endowed with exhaustive and explicit introspective access to his syntactic and lexical knowledge, then the correct grammar could be constructed "by dictation" from his testimony, independently of any reliance on the theorist's semantic intuitions *inter alia*. But of course there is no such speaker-hearer; the vast majority of our linguistic competence is opaque to introspection. Consequently, the theorist must often rely on what clues he can gather from his own and others' verbal and nonverbal behaviors, from his assessments of theoretical coherence and simplicity, and most importantly, from his own and others' linguistic intuitions—*semantic* as well as syntactic and lexical.

Let me emphasize how weak my present claim is. In particular, it does not concern the substance of the grammatical theory; I do not, for instance, mean to advocate a so-called generative semantics over a theory of autonomous syntax. Nor, furthermore, do I mean to deny the independent *specifiability* of syntactic and lexical structure; for all I have said, once the grammatical theory has been formulated, an exhaustively syntactic-cum-lexical description of any string can be provided. For example, 'keep' might be listed in the lexicon as a verb taking a noun phrase and a prepositional phrase (as in 'keep bikes in the shed'); 'keep tabs on' could then be listed separately as a particular instantiation of that same structure requiring 'tabs' as the relevant noun phrase and 'on' plus some noun phrase as the relevant prepositional phrase (Horrocks 1987, 50). Similarly, the theory might derive the sentence 'Harriet I spotted yesterday at the movies' from the sentence 'I spotted Harriet yesterday at the movies' by a so-called *movement* rule which moves the noun phrase 'Harriet' to initial position (Soames and Perlmutter 1979, 232). Only syntactic and lexical kinds need be invoked. My claim, rather, is that considerations of meaning are sometimes brought to bear in the theoretical isolation or discovery—not in the definition or constitution, nor in the *speaker-hearer's* "discovery"—of grammatical structures.[15]

The foregoing considerations suggest then that the linguistic meaning plays at least these two meta-theoretic roles vis-à-vis the theoretical postulation of grammatical structure. First and foremost, the speaker-hearer's recovery of meaning is the *explanandum* of the grammatical theory; call this 'the explanatory role'. Second, and as a result, the theorist's knowledge of meaning often serves to guide grammatical theory construction; call this 'the guiding role'. What I shall now try to show is that a precisely analogous situation obtains in the musical realm. That is to say, there is a musical feature that plays this same pair of roles and hence, for that reason together with some others I shall mention later on, may merit the name 'musical quasi-meaning'.

3.5 A Musical Parallel

What is the *explanandum* of the M-grammar? Well, musical understanding. And what is that? Lerdahl and Jackendoff have told us that musical understanding consists in having in your head a maximally coherent structural description of the music. But of course that cannot be right as it stands, for the unconscious structural description is what their theory *postulates*, not what it explains; in other words, the structural description is the *explanans*, not the *explanandum*, of their theory. Specifically, the unconscious structural description is proposed in order to explain something *observed*—namely, musical understanding. So the question is: what do we observe and seek to explain by postulating a structural description? The answer must be: the way the music sounds (to an experienced listener). We want to explain the having of conscious musical experience, musical feelings. Granted, we also observe various verbal and bodily behaviors—e.g., reports about what the meter is, about what the structurally important events are, about where the phrases begin and end, and so forth, along with foot tappings, whistlings, swayings to and fro, and the myriad bodily motions of the expressive performer—and the grammatical theory will presumably contribute to an explanation of these as well. But it is just obvious, I take it, that the latter *explananda* are secondary to our musical experience (indeed, at least some of them are presumably *effects* of it). Rather, we postulate the unconscious structural description in order to explain why the music sounds the way it does, why we have the characteristic feelings of beat strength, tonal center, harmonic tension, stability, relaxation, and the rest. Our having of this experience—this understanding—is the observed phenomenon we seek to explain.

Perhaps initially what's most striking here is the *difference* between music and language. To begin with, it is not entirely clear just what linguistic understanding is; for example, is it an ability? If so, an ability to do what, and under what circumstances? Or is it a state of having certain representations in your head? Or is it a conscious experience? Or some combination of these? (By the same token, what exactly is it that the L-grammatical theory is supposed to explain?) Moreover, if linguistic understanding either is or includes a conscious experience of some sort, does the experience have a phenomenal character or "quale"? Certainly there is a difference between, say, the experience of hearing Chinese when you don't understand it and the experience of hearing it when you do; but it's very difficult to say anything at all about what the experience of "hearing with understanding" is like. In short, if linguistic understanding has a phenomenology, it is hardly a salient one. Musical understanding, on the other hand, fairly glitters with "raw feels"; as Robert Kraut observes,

> understanding music is first and foremost a *phenomenological* matter: to understand a musical event is to hear it in certain ways. . . . One understands a musical event if and only if one experiences appropriate qualitative states in response to it (In press).

In this respect at least, musical and linguistic understanding seem very different indeed.[16]

At the same time, the similarities are equally striking. First of all, as in the linguistic case, if our having of musical feelings is the *explanandum* of the M-grammatical theory, then we should expect the theorist's knowledge of those feelings to guide grammatical theory construction. Indeed that is just what we find. Consider the following passages from Lerdahl and Jackendoff 1983, for example:

> For beats to be strong or weak there must exist a *metrical hierarchy*— two or more levels of beats. The relationship of "strong beat" to "metrical level" is simply that, if a beat is felt to be strong at a particular level, it is also a beat at the next larger level. In 4/4 meter, for example, the first and third beats are felt to be stronger than the second and fourth beats, and are beats at the next larger level; the first beat is felt to be stronger than the third beat, and is a beat at the next larger level; and so forth. Translated into the dot notation, these relationships [are indicated as follows:] at the smallest level of dots the first, second, third, and fourth beats are all beats; at the intermediate level there are beats under numbers 1 and 3; and at the largest level there are beats only under number 1 (19).

A similar dynamic can be seen in the construction of the prolongational reduction:

> In the grouping, metrical, and time-span components there is nothing that expresses the *sense of tension and relaxation* involved in the ongoing progress of music. . . . We wish to be able to speak

of points of relative tension and repose and the way music progresses from one to the other. This is the function of prolongational reduction (179). . . . We begin by defining tension and relaxation in terms of right and left prolongational branching. . . . [A] tensing motion will be represented by a right branch, a relaxing motion by a left branch (181; my emphasis).

As before, I do not mean to be making a claim about the substance of the grammatical theory; the M-grammatical rules themselves need make no mention of the feelings in question. Nor do I deny the independent specifiability of musical structure: once the grammatical theory is in place, we can perfectly well provide a purely formal or structural description of the music. (Indeed, the possibility of thus distinguishing musical structure from musical feelings only enhances the plausibility of casting the latter in a quasi-semantic role.) For instance, a strong beat, represented by a relatively large number of dots, is one that registers at relatively deep (global) levels in the structural description. A weak prolongation of one event by another, represented by a branching with a filled-in circle, is a structural relationship in which both events have the same root but the former event is represented at a deeper structural level and is in a more consonant position than the latter (1983, 182). The hierarchy of consonance and dissonance relations can in turn be specified in any format you please—even in a simple list. The completed M-grammar is, as advertised, a purely formal theory.

At this juncture, more must be said to delimit the class of feelings at issue, especially if my negative claims about the emotions are going to have any punch. Inevitably, its boundaries are fuzzy; but there are clear members, and clear nonmembers, and a sturdy rule of thumb, at least, for deciding membership in any particular case. In general, feelings merit inclusion in the explanatory-cum-guiding class insofar as it is plausible to suppose that they *could* play the relevant pair of roles vis-à-vis the theoretical assignment of musical structure.[17] Alternatively: feelings merit inclusion insofar as they either do play the relevant pair of roles or are *of a kind* with those that do. Alternatively still: feelings merit inclusion insofar as they can plausibly be viewed as constituting conscious experience or awareness—what we have been calling 'conscious knowledge'—of the content of the underlying structural description.

A look at the best grammatical theory will provide a good idea which feelings these are. For instance, in the Lerdahl-Jackendoff theory, Metrical Preference Rule 2 says "Weakly prefer a metrical structure in which the strongest beat in a group appears relatively early in the group" (1983, 76). As we have seen, beat strength is something the listener *feels*: for instance, "In 4/4 meter, the first and third beats are felt to be stronger than the second and fourth beats" (1983, 19). In other words, there is a characteristic "beat-strength feeling," as we might call it. Indeed, meter itself is felt: "It is the . . . regular alternation of strong and weak beats . . . that produces the *sensation* of meter" (1983, 69; my emphasis). Prolongational structure is said to underlie the tension and relaxation of the music; for example, a melodic descent from E-natural to C-natural over a C major triad "is felt as a relaxation . . . [b]ecause the second event is more 'consonant' [than the first]" (180).

It would be a mistake, however, to restrict the class in question to those feelings explicitly invoked in the construction and/or statement of the grammatical theory. Rather, we want to include feelings that are "relevantly similar to," or "of a kind with," those explicitly invoked in the theory. No doubt we shall typically defer to the music theorists and psychologists when a decision is required. For instance, what about feelings of tautness, peacefulness, and agitation? If tension, relaxation, and dissonance are in the bunch, why not these as well? Answer: No reason at all, provided it is plausible to suppose that they could play the explanatory and guiding roles. (Who knows what etymological odysseys have lead to our current use of 'tension' and 'relaxation' as opposed to 'tautness' and 'peacefulness'? For all we know, the experts would happily endorse a replacement throughout.) What must be decided is (for instance) whether the word 'tautness' can plausibly be applied to the feeling one experiences in hearing an acoustic event as a dominant seventh, or as a progression, or as a deceptive cadence.

Of course in some instances there may be no consensus, even among the experts. Disagreements should not worry us, however, for we expect the explanatory-cum-guiding class to admit some clear cases (e.g., musical tension and relaxation), some clear noncases (e.g., joy and sadness, I shall argue), and some borderline cases (e.g., tautness and peacefulness). A demand for sharp divisions is inappropriate here. Furthermore, I do not mean to suggest that it is always clear, or even always determinate, how a musical event or passage feels. Does a deceptive cadence "feel the same way" when it occurs in the opening statement of the theme as when it is embedded in a transitional passage in the development section? Does a melody "feel the same way" when stated at the octave? Do pitch-time events have a "core" feeling or "character" that remains invariant across changes in musical context? Can the same feeling be "expressed" by different musical strings, or does every distinct configuration of pitch-time events give rise to a distinct feeling? I do not have answers to these questions. Nor have I tried to supply a procedure for determining which feelings are the *correct* ones for a particular work. (See Kraut, in press, for help with that one.) Rather, my proposal concerns the *kind* of thing musical meaning is, in the present sense of the term, and might best be expressed this way: the meaning of a musical work consists in the feelings that result (or would result) from the experienced listener's unconscious recovery of structures constitutive of the work, *whatever those structures may be*.

3.6 Further Support: A Trio of Analogies

If what I have been saying is right, there is a roughly delimited class of peculiarly musical feelings (feelings of beat strength, metrical stress, prolongational tension, and so forth) that play the same explanatory and guiding roles with respect to the theoretical assignment of musical structure that the linguistic meanings play with respect to the assignment of linguistic structure. Of course, playing those roles is hardly sufficient for being a (quasi-)semantics; it is at most necessary, and is probably better viewed as "symptomatic" of semantic function. However, the musical feelings turn out to display certain other features that further enhance the plausibility of casting them in a quasi-semantic role. Here are three.

First, the identification of musical meanings with musical feelings gets a boost from the fact that, alone in his room with Wagner and Stravinsky, the experienced listener cannot help but understand; that is, he cannot help but have the relevant feelings. *This* brand of musical understanding is creative: the experienced listener can understand indefinitely many novel pieces of tonal music.[18] Second, if a listener fails to feel the C-natural in a C major scale as the most stable pitch in the collection, or a 4–3 suspension as a relaxation, or the downbeat as the strongest beat in the bar, then *ceteris paribus* he is mistaken: we will be justified in saying that he has misunderstood the music, that he ought to listen more carefully—or, perhaps, that he does not yet "know the language." However the determination of correctness is made, our musical feelings are the *kind* of thing to which the categories 'right' and 'wrong' can sensibly be applied. I shall return to this point in the next section when we consider some emotivist theories.

Third and last, our proposal lays the groundwork for an attractive theory of musical communication. If the musical feelings are musical quasi-meanings, then we may expect that just as linguistic meanings are communicated via the production and reception of linguistic strings, musical feelings are communicated via the production and reception of musical strings. A cognitivist like Jerry Fodor envisions linguistic communication in this way:

> Verbal communication is possible because, when [an acoustic object] U is a token of a linguistic type in a language [both speaker and hearer] understand, the production/perception of U can effect a certain kind of correspondence between the mental states of the speaker and the hearer. The ultimate goal of a theory of language is to say what kind of correspondence this is and to characterize the computational processes involved in bringing it about. . . . It may be worth emphasizing that this sort of account has a quite natural interpretation as a *causal* theory of communication. For if, as I have supposed, the utterance of a wave form can bring about a certain correspondence between the mental states of the speaker and the hearer, this is presumably because, in the relevant cases, the utterance is causally sufficient to initiate the sequence of psychological processes in the hearer which eventuates in his coming to be in a mental state that corresponds to the one that the speaker is in. . . . So, one might say, a necessary and sufficient condition for communication between speaker and hearer is that the mental states of the one should be in the right sort of causal relation to the mental states of the other (1975, 103–104).

One can imagine the communication of musical feelings proceeding in much the same manner, underwritten by a correspondence of musical representations in the minds of composer, performer, and listener.[19] On this view, what the performer (and, through him, the composer) communicates is his way of hearing the music, his way of feeling it. The performer's mission is to sculpt the nuances of pitch, duration, loudness, and the rest in such a way that his listeners feel the music in the same way he does. If he wants us to feel the phrase boundary at one place rather than another, he may slow down there, or perhaps pause for air; if he wants us to feel a certain passage in three rather than two, he may emphasize certain events by playing them louder, or longer, or by giving them stronger attacks. (See, e.g., Palmer 1989, Gabrielsson 1974, 1982, and Clarke 1987 for experimental confirmation.) A particular, idiosyncratic way of hearing or feeling a piece of music is the performer's "interpretation" of it, the "message" he means to communicate or express by his playing. Thus each performance affords the experienced listener an occasion to hear the work in a new way, to acquire further knowledge of it, to grasp more of its . . . meaning.

Lest there be any confusion: I do not mean to be arguing for a musical semantic "component" analogous to the hypothesized semantic component of the linguistic grammar. There is presumably no motivation for such rules as 'When a pair of pitch-time events is structurally described by a left branching in the prolongational reduction, have a feeling of relaxation'. That is as it should be, of course, for whereas the relation of a linguistic string to its meaning is a more or less conventional one, the relation of a musical string to the relevant feelings is nonconventional: we are presumably just *wired* in such a way as to have those feelings upon tokening those mental representations. Not surprisingly, the tie between music and feelings is considerably tighter than the tie between a sentence and its meaning.

In the final analysis, then, do the musical feelings constitute a quasi-semantics? I leave it to the reader to decide. If you require of any semantics, quasi or otherwise, that it specify truth conditions for well-formed strings, or that its values be established by convention, or that it be explicitly represented in the grammar of the language, then you will be inclined to answer in the negative. If on the other hand you are impressed by the fact that the musical feelings result in systematic ways from grammar-driven operations defined over representations of acoustic stimuli, are clearly distinguishable from those operations and the representations operated upon, are creative in Chomsky's sense, sustain robust notions of correctness and error (about which I shall say more in a moment), underwrite the beginnings of a plausible theory of musical communication, and play the explanatory and guiding roles characteristic of meaning in the natural language, then you may well answer in the affirmative. If "independent" musical meaning exists at all, these feelings lie at the heart of it.

3.7 Emotivist Semantics Reconsidered

I shall close with some negative remarks about the candidacy of the emotions for musical meanings. The literature on music cites a breath-taking assortment of states under the rubric of emotion. Just for ex-ample, a well-known psychological study by Hevner (1936) includes being merry, joyous, sad, pathetic, spiritual, lofty, dignified, dreamy, tender, and dramatic. Bell (1914) posits a special "aesthetic emotion," while Hanslick (1957) insists that music expresses not emotions *per se*, but rather their "dynamical properties"—the "speed, slowness, strength, weakness [etc.] . . . accompanying psychical action"(24).[20] At present I do not wish to become mired in the details of these various accounts. Rather, I want simply to urge that stereotypical emotions—happiness, sadness, anger, jealousy, and fear, for example—cannot play the musical semantic role often envisioned for them.

Ideally one would want to present a fully developed theory of the emotions, explaining precisely how they differ from the musical feel-ings discussed above; but I am not in a position to do that here.[21] For present purposes it will suffice to distinguish the two species of feeling by observing that, among other things, emotions appear to have a conative element that is absent from the musical feelings. Whereas an emotional state (at least typically) involves a positive or negative evaluation of some object or state of affairs, the musical feelings are neutral in this regard; feeling an event as tense or relaxed, metrically strong or weak, harmonically stable or unstable, does not seem to involve any evaluation of it. Furthermore, though of course I cannot prove so, it seems plausible to regard the musical feelings as essentially perceptual in nature—indeed, essentially *auditory;* whereas there is nothing peculiarly perceptual, *a fortiori* peculiarly auditory, about being happy or sad. No doubt there are further significant disparities, but I shall leave it at that for now. After all, a distinction between emotions and musical feelings is hardly tendentious; as Kraut observes,

> "[e]xpressivist" semantics, according to which music is somehow a vehicle for the expression of emotion, is implausible in connection with a wide range of music. Here the issue is perhaps terminological (what precisely is an emotion?); but caution is nevertheless required. Seasoned listeners rarely experience joy, jealousy, indignation, envy, love, fear, or other stereotypical emotions in response to up-tempo Ornette Coleman performances. Not every phenomenological episode corresponds to an emotion; there is more to emotion than feeling. The complex experiences and intricate sensory-perceptual states associated with such music cannot be assumed, pending further discussion, to constitute emotions (In press).

With this distinction in hand, then, let us see why emotions cannot be musical meanings.

The main problem is that emotions—by which I mean to include emotional responses to the music, emotive properties of the music, emotions supposedly expressed by the music, and so on—do not sustain the requisite normativity in the musical realm. Granted, if Schubert *tells* us that he means his quartet to signify terror, or if he is commissioned to write a terrifying work, then it seems reasonable to claim that terror is part of the meaning of the quartet and that a listener who fails to ascribe it that meaning fails to (completely) understand it. Similarly, there are good reasons to include death in the meaning of the Mozart *Requiem* and springtime in the meaning of *Le Sacre du Printemps.* But this dependent sort of meaning is clearly not what Scruton and other proponents of an emotive musical semantics have had in mind; in particular, it is not a meaning that can be grasped just by hearing the music. As Scruton would have it, emotive musical meaning is (at least part of) the *independent* meaning of a work; our understanding of it is *creative.* Recall his admirably unflinching claim: "No one can listen to this passage [of the Schubert quartet] without

instantly sensing the object of this terror."[22] Moreover, in Scruton's
view this independent emotive meaning of a piece is norm-governed:

> [S]omeone who described the last movement of *The Jupiter Sym-*
> *phony* as morose and life-negating would . . . be wrong, however
> clearly his judgment was founded in theory. For this description
> is something that cannot be heard in the music by a musically
> cultivated person (1987, 170).

Scruton's point, I take it, is a conceptual one: if you hear the *Jupiter* as
morose, you are *ipso facto* an incompetent listener, and the rest of us
need not take your assessment seriously. Likewise, if I listen to the
Schubert and find no emotional significance in it at all, or if I find it
beseeching, or just mildly unsettling, rather than terrifying, I am incompetent; I have misunderstood the work.

This is very hard to swallow, especially given the absence of any
explanation *how* the listener descries the emotive meaning of a piece
(cf. the passage from Scruton cited on p. 43). Furthermore, if some
philosophers believe in the possibility of emotive musical mistakes,
musicians certainly do not. Indeed, the musicians I have polled regard
the idea of such an emotional "mistake" as something of a *category*
mistake. A listener's emotional response to a work may surprise or
baffle us, of course: if he finds the Schubert jolly, for example, we may
wonder what he "hears in it." But we should no more call him mistaken
than the diner who prefers swordfish to salmon. I am not saying that
emotions *couldn't* sustain the relevant normativity, only that apparently they *do* not—at least not if we are going to put any stock in the
verbal behavior of musicians.

Nor are musicians the only ones whose intuitions run this way. Test
yours against the following example. Suppose a violinist (Arnold
Steinhardt, say) has played the Schubert many times, and, by all
standards, magnificently. Suppose furthermore that Steinhardt finds
the "terrifying" passage jolly. On what emotive ground could one deny
that he understands the music? Surely the character of his playing
(among other things) would overrule any such putative emotive evidence. Granted, *as a matter of psychological fact* it may turn out that giving a "maximally coherent" performance of the Schubert is perfectly
correlated with feeling (having in mind? intending to express?) terror;

and perhaps most or even all listeners do hear the relevant passage as terrifying. (Maybe the music processor sits near the affective centers in the brain, so that activation of the minor key nodes in the musical net spills over into the fear area. The situation might be that brute.) But even if that is all true (which I doubt), it does not underwrite the normativity required for meaning; in other words, it does not make terror the *correct* feeling. Emotional responses to music are neither correct nor incorrect—typical or atypical, perhaps, but not right or wrong.

To be sure, it is always open to us to dispute Steinhardt's phrasing, tempo, dynamics, articulations, and so forth; here, argument can take place, grounds can be summoned for one way of hearing or feeling the music as opposed to another. "No, the phrase ends *here*, because that E-natural is already preparing a modulation to the dominant!" (In other words, for example, "You are wrong to feel that E-natural as stable!" Compare: "No, the phrase ends here because that E-natural expresses terror!" Say the latter to a musician and see how far you get.) Such disputes may prove unresolvable, of course; indeed, impasses are common, presumably arising when listeners "hear the music differently" owing to disparities in their unconscious structural descriptions. But such disputes, far from undermining the normativity of the judgments at issue, are possible only in its presence. I shall not here attempt an explanation for the normativity of our musical feelings; no doubt their intimate affiliation with musical *structure* will loom large in any such account, but considerable work will be required to spell out the details.[23] For present purposes I take it as a datum that our musical feelings, unlike the emotional properties or effects of the music, are firmly lodged in a framework in which genuine dispute can and does occur. Musicians argue about phrasings and dynamics and resolutions. They do *not* argue about the emotions they feel or otherwise ascribe to the music.

Again, not for a moment do I wish to deny that we have emotional responses to, associate emotional experiences with, and ascribe emotive properties to, the music we hear. For example, there is some evidence to suggest that listeners can pair musical selections with "emotive" adjectives from predetermined lists (e.g., 'tender', 'buoyant', 'doleful') with a fair degree of consistency and intersubjective agreement.[24] In addition, I am inclined to think that Clive Bell got things very nearly right in proposing the existence of a peculiar aesthetic emotion; details of Bell exegesis aside, our experience of artworks is often characterized by a feeling whose content is expressible roughly as "Wow, to think that someone thought of this!" Such a sentiment must be broadly ethical in nature, "bringing men together," as Cavell says. I don't propose to delve into the psychology of our emotional responses to music or the ethical dimensions of aesthetic experience;[25] at present I want simply to acknowledge their obvious reality. My point, rather, is that neither the consistency, nor the intersubjective accord, nor the presumptive ethical function, nor *a fortiori* the mere reality of our emotive responses to music can underwrite the normativity required for meaning. On the contrary, the tacit rule is: In matters (musically) affective, to each his own.

At the beginning I remarked upon the ambiguity of 'meaning' as between, roughly, content and value. My suspicion is that some emotivist theories of musical meaning are spurred by a conflation of these two senses of the term. No doubt music *means* something to us, in the sense of being important or valuable, in part because of its emotive properties. Cavell says:

> [O]bjects of art not merely interest and absorb, they move us; we are not merely involved with them, but concerned with them, and care about them; we treat them in special ways, invest them with a value which normal people otherwise reserve only for other people...They *mean* something to us, not just the way statements do, but the way people do (1967, 84).

Perhaps the valuing of musical works for their emotive properties, in concert with their apparent possession of grammatical structure, fosters the mistaking of those emotive properties for musical *contents*. And of course, if I am right, then the quasi-meanings of musical works *are* feelings—just not the kind that proponents of emotivist theories have traditionally had in mind.

3.8. Looking Ahead

The query that prompted these reflections concerned the specialness of musical artworks, in particular our attention to the "feeling" ineffability in our knowledge of them. My suggestion was that music's grammatical structure creates the expectation of a semantics—something effable. What we get instead are the ineffable musical feelings of tonicity, beat strength, tension, resolution, stability, and so forth, the experiencing of which constitutes our conscious knowledge or understanding of the music. On the picture I am tendering, then, the yield of grammatical processing in language and music alike is *knowledge* or *understanding*—a.k.a. the grasp of *meaning*; it's just that in the musical case the knowledge is ineffable: it is sensory-perceptual or felt in nature and hence not communicable by language *ab initio*. This ineffability violates our semantic expectations, and so we notice it. I then went on to suggest that the musical feelings, though not a semantics strictly speaking, may reasonably be viewed as an analogue to a semantics—a quasi-semantics. (Shades of Kant's purposiveness without a purpose, perhaps, in a very different suit of clothing.)

The so-called feeling ineffability is a more robust ineffability than the structural kind, but it too leaves something to be desired. As we have heard, once the requisite longterm schemas are in place (and we shall hear more about those in the next chapter), trained listeners can communicate their knowledge of the music *by language*. Or, more properly, they can communicate their knowledge of the *structural* features of the music by language—which brings me to an important clarification. Throughout this chapter I have focused on the structural features of the music, specifically on their hypothesized role in the fostering of semantic "expectations." Strictly speaking, though, the feeling ineffability attaches to our knowledge of the nonstructural features as well; knowledge of both kinds of features is sensory-perceptual or felt knowledge. However, as we shall soon see, whereas knowledge of the structural features can be communicated by language provided the requisite schemas are in place, knowledge of (at least some of) the nonstructural features cannot be communicated by language under any circumstances. The latter features can be known only, as it were, by acquaintance.[26] To that extent they are "more ineffable" than the structural features; they are, as I shall put it, *nuance* ineffable.

Over the course of the next two chapters we shall examine our knowledge of the nonstructural features of the music, which alone sustains the last, and the hardiest, of the three ineffabilities. Happily, we can continue to use Cavell's remarks as a beacon. I shall suggest that the passages from "Music Discomposed" (cited on p. 1 above) admit a second interpretation that is importantly different from the one we have tracked so far. Notice Cavell's repeated use of the gerundive constructions 'in sensing' and 'in feeling': works of art are only known *in sensing* or *in feeling*. Such locutions hint at something stronger than the claim that knowledge of artworks is sensory-perceptual or felt knowledge; specifically, they seem to suggest that knowledge of artworks is an occurrent phenomenon, as if a work is known only *while being* sensed or felt. In what follows we shall discover just such a brand of occurrent musical knowledge—one that turns out, not surprisingly, to be a well-spring of ineffability. First, though, I shall need to say more about the distinction between structural and nonstructural features of the music.[27]

Chapter 4
A Psychology of Musical Nuance

The distinction between a philosophical and a psychological theory is heuristic: a quick way of indicating which kinds of constraints are operative in motivating a given move in theory construction....I am morally certain that real progress will be made by researchers with access to an armamentarium of argument styles that considerably transcends what any of the traditional disciplines has to offer. That, despite frequent lapses into mere carnival, is what is hopeful about the recent interest in developing a cognitive science.

Jerry Fodor 1981a, 19

If Fodor is right about the Renaissance prerequisites for doing cognitive science, here is where we will feel the pressure. I'll try to keep the presentation as clear and as simple as possible, but still there are fine points of music theory and psychology that must be grasped if the promised account of the nuance ineffability is to persuade. The good news is that with chapter 4 (and the first part of chapter 5) behind us we shall once again find ourselves in familiar philosophical territory, and the hard work will reward.

First, several policy statements. (1) Unless I indicate otherwise, the arguments of the next two chapters will refer exclusively to the musical dimension of *pitch*. This strategy owes to two simple and theoretically uninteresting facts—viz., that most of the studies germane to our project happen to concern pitch, and that pitch is what I know the most about. So let me emphasize at the outset that any conclusions drawn herein, if correct, should apply *mutatis mutandis* to other relevantly similar properties of the music. (Just which ones count as relevantly similar will emerge as we go along.) (2) Unless I indicate otherwise, the hypothetical listener invoked below will be a trained listener lacking

so-called *perfect pitch*.[1] (I have been supposing this all along but hadn't
said so until now.) Since relatively little is known about the latter
ability, and since in any case I am not presently interested in how a
listener so endowed might or might not differ from the ordinary trained
listener, I shall restrict the scope of my claims accordingly: if the listener
with perfect pitch differs from the ordinary trained listener in ways
relevant to the issue of ineffable knowledge (which I doubt), then my
account does not apply to him. (3) Lastly, there is the familiar and
inevitable shakiness of inferences from what goes on in the lab to what
goes on *in rerum naturae*. Many of the experiments pertinent to our
investigation employ synthesized sine tones (i.e., tones lacking the
overtones inherent in any instrumental or vocal tone), and stimuli are
often presented independently of any tonal or otherwise musical context. Things have improved recently with the development of a cognitive psychology of music, but in many cases there is still no alternative
but to rely on data obtained under these impoverished conditions. (For
ease of discussion, I shall often refer to such data as 'artificial'.) Where
there exist no data (artificial or otherwise) bearing on a given issue, I
shall extrapolate from closely allied data, from current psychological
theory, and from my own musical experience.

   With caveats, policies, and apologies out of the way, let us turn to
the topic at hand.

4.1 Structural vs. Nonstructural Representations

As must by now be clear, the rules of the M-grammar range first and
foremost over what I'll call 'chromatic pitch-time events'—or, since
we'll be talking exclusively about pitch, 'chromatic pitch-events', or
'C-pitch-events' for short. These are acoustic events considered as
tokens of the twelve chromatic pitch (C-pitch) types A-natural, B-flat,
B-natural, and so forth. Accordingly, in any given real-time hearing of
a tonal work, the input to the M-grammatical rules is (for all intents
and purposes) a representation of incoming acoustic events as instantiating the sequence of pitches specified in the score.[2] Simply put: in
real-time hearing, the input to the M-grammar is a mental recovery of
the score. Call this the *mental score*.

   As we learned in chapter 2, the mental score is already the result of
inferences from transduced representations of acoustic frequencies; in

other words, the M-grammatical rules are not effective "from the bottom."[3] Now you might suppose that the mental score is inferred *directly* from transducer outputs, making it the shallowest level of representation to whose content the listener has conscious access. But if that were so, there would be no way to explain how we consciously hear "within-category" phenomena such as vibrato,[4] slides, out-of tune intervals, and the myriad shades of pitch coloration that distinguish one performance from another. Robison's C-sharps may be slightly lower than Dwyer's, or Steinhardt's D-sharps a shade higher than his E-flats;[5] DuPré may narrow her vibrato in tense passages and widen it in relaxed ones, while Rampal's E-naturals tend to be slightly flat in the middle register. These fine-grained details of a performance—these *nuances*—are features the score does not (indeed *cannot*) dictate, hence precisely the sorts of features the performer can manipulate in forging his peculiar interpretation of a musical work.

We shall learn more about performance nuances as our story develops, but for now the important point is this: in hearing these nuances, we are hearing differences within—that is, more fine-grained than—the C-pitch and C-interval (chromatic interval) categories. Each C-pitch category subsumes many discriminably different pitches, just as each "determinable" color category subsumes many different "determinate" shades; there are many A-naturals and many B-flats, just as there are many reds and many blues. Under laboratory conditions of minimal uncertainty, the human ear can discriminate anywhere from 20 to 300 pitches to the semitone, depending upon the frequency range and testing procedure employed (e.g., Burns and Ward 1982, 244).[6] Despite the unavoidably artificial character of such a finding, it gives us good reason to expect that listeners can discriminate multiple pitches to the semitone even in real-time music perception, where stimulus uncertainty and complexity are assumed to be high. (For that matter, the succeeding discussion will give us reason to doubt that real-time musical stimuli *are* of high uncertainty; more on that in §4.3.) Thus we may suppose that whereas score and mental score alike can specify tokens of twelve octave-equivalent C-pitch types, we actually *hear* many more than twelve different pitches in a typical performance. Let us call these many fine-grained determinate pitches 'nuance pitches', or 'N-pitches' for short.

Similarly, each C-interval category (see again note 6) subsumes many discriminably different intervals; just as we hear many different A-naturals and B-flats, we hear many different perfect fourths and major sixths. Perhaps the most familiar examples of within-category intervals are intervals that are out-of-tune—that is, intervals that are too wide or too narrow relative to the correct width for their respective interval categories. (In such cases we can say either that the interval is out-of-tune or that one or both of its constituent pitches are; these are effectively just different ways of saying the same thing. For a pitch to be out-of-tune [viz. sharp or flat] is for it to be too high or too low relative to the correct width for the interval of which it is a constituent; thus pitches are in- or out-of-tune only relative to their *distances* from other pitches.) Not all interval nuances derive from errors of intonation or tuning, however. Many fine-grained differences in interval width—indeed the most interesting and important ones, for our purposes—are fully intended *expressive* features, as when a flutist ever so slightly raises ("sharpens") an F-sharp sustained over a D-natural across a modulation from b minor to D major, or a singer slides languorously from the leading tone to the tonic at the final cadence of a melody. The flutist's objective is to widen ("brighten") the major third between D-natural and F-sharp, thereby emphasizing and strengthening the new key of D major, while the singer's objective is to shrink the semitone between leading tone and tonic, thereby delaying the sense of resolution at the end.

The data on interval discrimination are somewhat obscure (more on that shortly), but discrimination thresholds for musical intervals appear to range from about one sixth-tone to one twentieth-tone (e.g., Burns and Ward 1978, 456; a sixth-tone is one third, and a twentieth-tone one tenth, the size of a semitone.). In other words, listeners can discriminate among (e.g.) perfect fourths that differ in width by anywhere from one sixth-tone to one twentieth-tone. Again, this datum was obtained under minimal-uncertainty conditions in the lab; but taken together with a moment's reflection on the character of real-time musical experience—we do, after all, hear out-of-tune intervals all the time—it lends strong support to the claim that we hear many more than twelve intervals to the octave. Call these fine-grained intervals 'nuance intervals', or 'N-intervals' for short.[7] (Readers concerned about the categorical perception of musical intervals are asked to be patient; that issue is treated at some length in §4.3.)

Let me emphasize that I do not intend the distinction between pitch and interval nuances, as characterized above, to be exhaustive even within the domain of pitch *überhaupt;* indeed, the existence of further kinds of pitch and/or interval nuances would only strengthen the line I shall take here. Moreover, it may be that pitch and interval nuances are recovered at distinct levels of representation in real-time hearing; in the terminology of chapter 2, the category 'N-interval' may be more abstract than the category 'N-pitch', so that N-intervals are represented at a deeper level in the listener's inferential series. For simplicity's sake, however, I shall suppose that all of the pitch and interval nuances are recovered at the same level; no damage to my view will result should this supposition prove false.

Be the details as they may, our conscious perception of N-pitches and N-intervals in a musical performance indicates that the mental score is inferred from a still shallower level of representation at which these fine-grained within-category values are recovered. Since this inference must be effected before the rules of the M-grammar can be engaged, with the result that the nuances are not captured in the structural description, their recovery is aptly termed a nongrammatical or *nonstructural* representation of the musical signal (see again §2.2). I shall call this nonstructural level of representation, comprising the N-pitch and N-interval representations, the 'nuance level', or 'N-level' for short. The N-level is presumably the shallowest (hence most "raw") representation of the signal to whose content the listener has conscious access.

Here then is the picture that emerges. The incoming musical signal is initially recovered as a sequence of proximal stimulations to the auditory transducers, where the transducer output is (for all practical purposes) a function of acoustic frequency. From this transduced representation is then inferred a representation of the signal as instantiating a sequence of N-pitches and N-intervals—namely, an N-level. From the N-level in turn is inferred a mental score, at which point the rules of the M-grammar are engaged and a structural description is assigned. Thus the mental score—the shallowest *grammatical* level of representation—is already an abstraction from a still shallower level at which the nonstructural nuance values are recovered. Relatively little attention has been paid to the N-level in the psychological literature, but as we are about to see, it enjoys a starring role in a cognitivist account of ineffable musical knowledge.

4.2 Interval Schemas: Psychological Go-Betweens

The mental score isn't lifted from the N-level by magic. How exactly is this shallowest grammatical representation constructed?

In presenting the time-span and prolongational components of the M-grammar (§2.2), I touched briefly on the hypothesized role of standing pitch representations or *schemas* in music perception. You may remember that Lerdahl and Jackendoff did not elucidate the nature of these mental structures, nor was there any pressing need for them to do so. We, however, will need to acquaint ourselves with schemas in some detail, for they play a major part in the construction of the mental score.

John Anderson (1980) explains:

> Schemas are large, complex units of knowledge that organize much of what we know about general categories of objects, classes of events, and types of people (128). . . . A schema is a much larger piece of knowledge than an image or proposition; it might be thought of as equivalent to a set of propositions and images. . . . [A] schema is general rather than specific (133).

A schema can be anything from a representation of the set of features typically possessed by birds (viz. wings, beak, legs, feathers, etc.) to a representation of the series of actions typically occurring during dinner at a restaurant (Schank and Abelson 1977). Schematic knowledge may assume any of a variety of forms; for example, knowledge of the bird features might be stored in a simple list, or in a template, or in some sort of multidimensional map, or in any number of other arrangements. Schemas are frequently conceived as networks in which "nodes" or "units" representing items of significance are linked together in various ways. In general, the thought is that a stimulus is recognized (type-identified) or "understood" to the extent that it is determined to have the features specified in the relevant list, or maps into the relevant template, or "activates" the relevant node in a network, and so forth. These enduring representations are commonly envisioned as a means of reducing information load by organizing (formerly, "chunking") an otherwise blooming and buzzing confusion of stimuli into various categories.

Many schemas, including musical ones, are thought to be hierarchically organized; it appears that the efficient and lasting storage of information is greatly facilitated by its hierarchical ordering. The dimension along which tonal musical schemas are stratified is typically that of stability, as J. J. Bharucha (1984a) explains:

> The tonal hierarchies used in Western music are the 12 major and minor keys. . . . These hierarchies are internalized by members of a culture, and facilitate the processing of music of that culture. The cognitive structure that incorporates information about a particular tonal hierarchy and uses this information to influence the encoding of music may be thought of as a tonal schema (486). . . . A tonal schema specifies a hierarchy of stability (a tonal hierarchy) of all possible [pitches] and chords (489).

Bharucha hypothesizes that in being exposed repeatedly to pieces of tonal music, the listener begins unconsciously to establish lasting mental structures that represent certain institutionalized relationships obtaining among the pitches, intervals, chords, and keys instantiated in those pieces. By 'institutionalized' I mean to emphasize the shared and systematic nature of these tonal relations: not peculiar to single pieces, they are rather constitutive of a whole musical genre (namely, Western tonal music), just as the institutional features of English are to be distinguished from the "idiolects" of particular novels or poems. Once established, the mental schemas that represent these relationships are mobilized in subsequent music perception. Very roughly, the thought is that the music processor brings (a representation of) the incoming signal into register with the tonal schemas, thereby transforming a chaotic manifold of unrelated pitch sensations into the perception of a differentiated and coherent sequence of intervals, chords, melodies, cadences, and so on.[8]

In Bharucha's connectionist model for the perception of harmonic structure, for example, "input" units representing the twelve C-pitches[9] are linked in various ways to units representing the chords and keys in which those pitches figure. Audition of a musical signal initially activates the input units, which activation in turn spreads via the relevant links to related chord and key units. The resulting pattern of activation over the network determines the listener's "expectancies" for harmonies to come:

> People exposed to Western music are assumed to acquire a network representation of [chords] and their organization in the form of keys, which serves to schematize subsequent perception. . . . The pattern of activation of key units represents the degree to which keys are established. Tonal music will tend to build up activation in one region of the network, such that one key unit is most highly activated, with activation tapering off with increasing distance from the focal key. Atonal music will typically induce a less focussed pattern. . . . The pattern of activation of chord units represents the pattern of expectancies for chords to follow. A chord whose unit is highly activated is strongly expected (1987b 512).

To come finally to my central point, schemas representing the twelve C-intervals, realized implicitly in Bharucha's network by the twelve C-pitch input units, appear to be of prime importance in the construction of the mental score from the N-level. (For simplicity's sake I shall restrict the present discussion to mental scores for melodies; the extrapolation to multi-voiced music should be straightforward.) Results of a study by Roger Shepard and Daniel Jordan (1984) suggest how the process might go. Shepard and Jordan model a diatonic scalar schema as a template into which a representation of the incoming stimulus is mapped:

> Diverse phenomena of perception and memory indicate that our experience is determined by internal schemata as well as by external inputs. Thus musical tones, though physically variable along a continuum of frequency, tend to be interpreted categorically as the discrete notes (named *do, re, mi, fa, sol, la, ti, do*) of an internalized musical scale. We suggest that the interval schema may act as a template that, when brought into register with a tonal input, maps the . . . physical tones into the discrete steps of the schema, with a resulting unique conferral of tonal stabilities . . . on the tones (1984, 1333).[10]

Fascinatingly, Shepard and Jordan found that the steps of an equalized octatonic scale (i.e., an eight-tone scale whose successive tones were separated by steps of logarithmically equal width) were heard as varying in width depending on their location relative to the (*unequal*) steps of a diatonic major scale; in particular, the step between the third and fourth tones in the equalized scale, and that between the seventh and eighth tones, though physically identical in width to the other steps, were heard as being relatively larger than the others.[11] The authors hypothesize that the steps in question were "judged larger because those two intervals [were] wide in relation to the narrower gaps 'expected' by the input template" (1333). Evidence also emerged to suggest that in some cases listeners unconsciously slide their scalar templates up and down (and perhaps also stretch and shrink them) to achieve the best possible fit with their representation of an incoming stimulus. For example, a stretched octatonic scale (here, an eight-tone scale that preserved the diatonic pattern of unequal scale steps but spanned a minor ninth instead of an octave) was heard as spanning only an octave; as a result, a tone one semitone above the original starting tone, sounded subsequently to the playing of the stretched scale, was misidentified as the original starting tone. Such a finding suggests that "the entire template had been shifted [upward] by approximately a half-tone" (1334).

The implication of the Shepard and Jordan data for our project is clear: it is plausible to suppose that the inference from N-level to mental score proceeds via a mapping of the N-level into a schema representing the twelve C-intervals. The interval schema is probably a chromatic scalar schema (as in Bharucha's network model, for instance)—a kind of grid, or a set of mental cubbyholes if you like, through which the N-level is passed. The grid is only as fine-grained as the C-intervals (i.e., the smallest step it installs between pitches is a semitone), so that the pitches represented in the N-level are categorized only that finely. Granted, Shepard and Jordan are testing rather special cases of schema-driven processing, but projecting to a schema for the twelve C-intervals, and to real musical signals as well as their distorted scalar sequences, should be straightforward enough.

The idea, then, is that a heard melody is mentally represented first and foremost as a sequence of C-intervals; in other words, it is represented, first and foremost, *relationally*. For example, your mental score for a performance of *The Star-Spangled Banner* will specify not a sequence of C-pitches *per se* (e.g. 'G, E, C, E, G, C, etc. ') but rather the sequence of *intervals* 'descending minor third, descending major third, ascending major third, etc.', or perhaps the sequence of scale degrees '5, 3, 1, 3, 5, 8, etc.' (After all, what's essential to *The Star-Spangled Banner*, like virtually any tonal work, is a sequence of pitch relationships or distances, not pitches *per se*; witness the fact that it can be played, and easily recognized, in any of the twelve diatonic major keys.[12]) I do not mean to claim, of course, that in hearing a performance of the national anthem you hear no particular C-pitches; the tune has to be played in some key or other, after all. Rather, my point is that what transforms your N-level into a mental score is the representation of incoming acoustic events as instantiating certain *relationships*—specifically, relationships of the kind embodied in your C-interval schema.[13] N.B. This is not to suggest that the N-pitch and N-interval information contained in the shallower N-level is lost altogether in the process: though the mental score is informationally impoverished compared to the N-level, the contents of both levels are "carried up" into the conscious percept. Thus conscious perception of a musical performance includes conscious perception not only of its structural features, but also of its fine, and not so fine, within-category nuances.

So far so good. What has the distinction between these two shallow levels of representation got to do with a theory of musical ineffability? As we heard in chapter 2, the trained listener can report the C-pitches he consciously hears in a musical signal (along, in principle, with the various deeper musical structures); in other words, the conscious content of his mental score—which just *is* his conscious knowledge of the C-pitches—is entirely (structurally) effable. However, I have yet to explain how such reports are made; that is, I have yet to explain how the listener derives the names of the specific C-pitches from their intervallic representation in his mental score. That will be my task in the final section of this chapter. Then, in chapter 5, I shall argue that our knowledge of the nuances of a musical performance differs from our knowledge of its structural features in a respect crucial to the possibility of verbal report. If I am right, our knowledge of the N-pitches and N-intervals is (nuance) ineffable: we have conscious knowledge of these nuances but cannot say which nuances they are.

Before turning to the anatomy of verbal report, however, I must pause here to address a concern that will by now be troubling any reader well-versed in the psychology of music—viz., the degree to which our perception of musical intervals is *categorical*.

4.3 Categorical Perception: Are We Deaf to Interval Nuances?

A significant body of psychological research suggests that under conditions of high stimulus uncertainty, the trained listener's perception of musical intervals is *categorical*. Strictly speaking, stimuli of a given kind are perceived categorically insofar as (1) subjects' identification functions with respect to those stimuli are step-like, reflecting sharp and reliable category boundaries, and (2) subjects' ability to discriminate among the stimuli is limited by (i.e., is no better than) their ability to type-identify them; in short, subjects are unable to detect within-category differences.[14] (In the present instance, the claim will be that listeners cannot discriminate among intervals within the C-interval categories.) Therefore, where perception is categorical, stimuli differing by a uniform amount along some relevant physical dimension (like frequency ratio) may be differentially distinguishable depending on whether they lie in the same category or in different categories. As Burns and Ward (1978) explain, categorical perception is characterized by

> discrimination "troughs" (near chance-level performance) for stimuli which lie well within identification category boundaries, as well as discrimination peaks for stimuli which lie across category boundaries. The implication is that categorical perception involves not merely a sharpening of discrimination across category boundaries, but an actual inability to use other than labeling information as a basis for discrimination (457).

Categorical perception "in the ideal," as defined above, almost never occurs; within-category discrimination is virtually always somewhat better than would be predicted from the relevant identification functions (e.g., Burns & Ward 1977, 457). Moreover, various adjustments to a given task design may increase or decrease the extent to which categorical perception occurs. For instance, *ceteris paribus* increases in stimulus uncertainty and memory load appear to increase the probability that perception will be categorical, whereas sufficient practice at within-category discrimination under minimal-uncertainty conditions can eradicate categorical perception altogether (see, e.g., Watson and Kelly 1981, Burns and Ward 1978). Intuitively speaking, categorical perception makes things easier for a perceptual processing system by allowing it to ignore fine-grained differences among the various instances of a given category. Categorical perception is contrasted with so-called *continuous* perception, which is characterized by smooth monotonic discrimination functions and, hence, within-category discrimination that far surpasses identification. (The perception of pitch, as opposed to intervals, appears to be more or less continuous in nature.)

   Evidence for the categorical perception of musical intervals derives from subjects' performance in at least two kinds of experimental tasks. First, it turns out that under laboratory conditions of high stimulus uncertainty, trained listeners can discriminate among presented intervals little better than they can type-identify or categorize them—and that, as we shall learn in some detail in chapter 5, is only as finely as tokens of the twelve C-interval types.[15] On the widespread assumption that stimulus uncertainty is high in real-time musical contexts, it is then hypothesized that real-time musical interval perception is categorical (e.g., Burns and Ward 1978, 466). Second, Siegel and Siegel (1977) have found that musicians are surprisingly inept at judging whether intervals (heard in isolation) are in-tune or out:

> [C]ategorical perception is shown by a tendency to call the stimuli 'in tune' roughly 80% of the time, regardless of whether the intervals are flat, sharp, or in tune (404). . . . [Subjects] apparently heard [virtually] all examples of a musical category as equivalent, as good examples of a standard musical interval (402).

Strictly speaking, judgments about tuning are (type) *identifications* of single presented stimuli (as opposed to discriminations among two or more presented stimuli). Categorical perception, on the other hand, is manifested in the character of our *discriminations*: where perception is categorical, discrimination is limited by identification. Nevertheless, it is easy to see why a claim of categorical perception can be inferred from the identification data that Siegel and Siegel obtained. In judging that a presented interval is in-tune (/wide/narrow), one is presumably judging that its width is *identical to* (/*greater than/less than*) the width specified by some internal standard (here we are supposing a C-interval schema); one is, as it were, "comparing" the presented interval to one's internal standard. Hence intervals that are judged severally to be in-tune are effectively judged to be identical to one another in width; and insofar as the listeners in the Siegel and Siegel study judged most of the intervals they heard to be in-tune, that amounts to their having heard most of the intervals in any given category as identical.

Extrapolating to real-time perception, Siegel and Siegel cite our apparent tolerance for notes that are strictly (i.e., acoustically) speaking out-of-tune:

> Common sense suggests ... that good musical performance is characterized at the very least by an accurate rendition of the notes in the written score. In fact, acoustic measurements of performances by well-known artists indicate a high degree of variability, similar to that found in speech. It is only because of ... categorical perception that we are largely unaware of the gross pitch deviations that are the norm in musical performance.... In music, categorical perception allows one to recognize the melody, even when the notes are out-of-tune, and to be blissfully unaware of the poor intonation that is characteristic of good musical performance (1977, 406-407).

The threat to my account of the nuance ineffability is clear: if the authors cited above are correct, then for all intents and purposes *we do not hear N-intervals* in real-time music perception. We hear minor sixths and perfect fourths all right, but we make no more fine-grained discriminations. This would not be so devastating a result if my case could rest comfortably on the N-pitches alone—pitch perception, recall, is supposed to be noncategorical or continuous. However, it seems likely that most of the nuances we hear in a performance are interval nuances; most of the time we are hearing "relationally," as it were, for it is in the relationships among the pitches of a performance that its *structure* consists. Thus my story of the nuance ineffability would be, if not entirely hobbled by our deafness to interval nuances, at least greatly weakened by it. How am I to respond here?

The first thing to realize is that, even if real-time perception of musical intervals is to some extent categorical, the effect is far less pervasive than Burns and Ward and Siegel and Siegel (among others) have imagined. I say this because it is obvious that we just *do* hear out-of-tune playing all the time; and we hear it in systematic, inter- and intra subjectively uniform, easily testable ways. We spend lots of time and money getting our instruments and voices properly tuned; musicians lose their jobs for playing out-of-tune! If we cannot discern whether intervals are in-tune or out, what on earth is the orchestra doing for 2 to 3 minutes at the beginning of every rehearsal and concert? Merely warming up? Showing off? I take it the point is clear: the claim that "musicians can't tell sharp from flat" in real-time music perception (Siegel and Siegel 1977, 399) is at best vastly overstated.

My suspicion is that, *contra* standard psychological doctrine, stimulus uncertainty is actually lower (i.e., predictability is actually higher) in many real-time musical contexts than in the corresponding experimental ones. Whereas the experimental stimuli are presented apart from any tonal or otherwise musical context, the highly structured context of a tonal work permits the generation of various expectancies ("predictions") that appear to enhance the listener's perception of fine-grained details. Crudely: *ceteris paribus* the more strongly a musical context "implies" an event of a certain kind (a certain pitch or harmony or rhythmic pattern, for example), the stronger the listener's expectation for that kind of event; the stronger his expectation, the more his attention is directed toward the expected event; and the more his attention is so directed, the more likely he is to notice any deviation from what he expects. To cite an especially relevant example, Bharucha and Stoeckig (1986) have obtained data suggesting that harmonic expectancies can enhance the listener's sensitivity to intonational errors (out-of-tuneness). Subjects in their study heard two major chords on each trial—first a "prime," and then a "target" to be judged. Sometimes the target chord was harmonically related to the prime, sometimes unrelated; sometimes the target was in-tune, sometimes out-of-tune by one eighth-tone. The subjects' task was to judge whether the target chord was in-tune or out. Overall, subjects were faster and more accurate in their judgments when the target was related to the prime than when it was unrelated—the hypothesis being that intonational sensitivity was heightened in the former condition because subjects were "primed" by the prime chord to expect chords related to it. (See also Bharucha 1987a.)

Nor are harmonic expectancies the only ones effective in this manner. Summarizing the results of a number of recent studies, Mari Riess Jones and William Yee (in press) report that

> temporal pattern context influences [pitch] discrimination. . . . Kidd et al. (1984) . . . used a standard and comparison task in which listeners indicated whether or not a 10-tone comparison sequence was identical to its standard when half the time it contained a small pitch change in one tone. Performance was best when both standard and comparison were isochronous; it declined when one or both were anisochronous and with increased uncertainties associated with the number and types of rhythms listeners heard in a session . . . [Also,] standard pattern rhythms can direct listeners' attention toward or away from the temporal location of a target tone in the comparison, leading to respectively good or poor discrimination of changes in target tone pitch (Jones et al. 1982) (26).

In these rhythm studies, the pitch changes at issue were greater than or equal to a semitone (i.e., they were not microtonal or within-category changes). Nevertheless, there is every reason to suppose that the kind of perceptual enhancement observed therein will generalize to the discrimination of microtonal pitch changes as well. The point is: apprehension of rhythmic regularities tends to heighten the listener's sensitivity to pitch differences *in general*.

Extrapolating from such findings, then, we may reasonably expect that the formation of various structural expectancies or "attentional sets" enhances the listener's sensitivity to fine-grained (within-category) differences among the intervals in a musical performance.[16] Intuitively speaking, tonal musical stimuli are always heard against the backdrop of a richly structured (if elastic) mental grid—auditory graph paper, one might say. That is why, when our attention is properly focused, we are often very good at hearing small differences among pitches and intervals *inter alia*: in the perception of a tonal work, we are surrounded by familiar auditory landmarks, anchor points relative to which we can gauge our current "position" along a variety of musical dimensions.[17]

I do not mean to suggest that the advocates of categorical interval perception are wholly mistaken. If it's obvious that we often hear fine-grained intonational deviations in a performance, it is equally obvious that we often fail to notice huge variations in interval size. (No doubt the malleability of our interval schemas is effective in the latter regard; see again Shepard and Jordan 1984.) Evidently real-time musical interval perception is sometimes categorical and sometimes not. If cognitively driven musical expectancies are indeed a determining factor, then we should not be surprised to find that *ceteris paribus* perception is less categorical for familiar music than for unfamiliar music, for tonal music than for atonal music, for largely "diatonic" music (e.g., Telemann or Vivaldi) than for highly "chromatic" music (e.g., Brahms or Scriabin), and for so-called "formulaic" music (e.g., Mozart minuets) than for "nonformulaic" music (e.g., Wagner operas), among other things. (Of course any such prediction is an empirical one and will need to be tested.)

No doubt myriad factors influence the character of real-time music perception (categorical vs. continuous), but I will not speculate further on those here. Be the details as they may, the important point for our purposes is this: if what I have been saying about real-time perception is correct, then it seems plausible to suppose that our apprehension of intervallic nuances is sometimes at least as fine-grained in music as it is in experimental tasks that do *not* elicit categorical perception (e.g., minimal uncertainty discrimination tasks).[18] Data obtained from such experiments indicate intervallic discrimination thresholds ranging from roughly one sixth-tone to one twentieth-tone (e.g., Burns and Ward 1978, 456); that is to say, the data indicate that listeners can recognize intervals as being out-of-tune by anywhere from one sixth-tone to one twentieth-tone. And again, that's in the lab—add a highly structured and perhaps familiar tonal context and it becomes entirely reasonable to suppose that our real-time perception of musical intervals is fine-grained indeed. In any case, the worst that could happen is that the interval nuances will turn out to be bigger than I have contended—in other words, that an interval will need to be out-of-tune by more than one sixth- to one twentieth-tone in order for us to hear the deviation. That we do hear within-category differences in interval width is a *datum*. Hence either way, whether I am right or whether I am wrong about the specific factors shaping the character of real-time hearing, our perception of interval nuances is secure.

4.4 Back To Our Story: Reporting the C-pitches

With worries about categorical perception laid to rest, let us retrieve the thread of our earlier discussion. We were wondering how the trained listener derives the names of the C-pitches of a heard melody from their intervallic (or scale degree) representation in his mental score. By this time the answer will seem refreshingly straightforward. We begin by looking at a network model of semantic knowledge.

In cognitivist corners, knowing the meaning of a word consists, like so much else, in having certain enduring representations in your head. An especially clear illustration is provided by John Anderson's *propositional network* (1980), which contains a model of the mental lexicon for English. According to Anderson, knowing the meaning of a word involves representing it in a network of interconnected nodes. For instance, knowing what 'apple' means consists (partly) in having a node for the category or kind APPLE linked in the right sorts of ways to nodes for the categories RED, GREEN, YELLOW, FRUIT, FOOD, and EAT, among others, and to a node for the word 'apple'. (Anderson calls the category nodes 'concepts'.) I say 'partly' because, as Anderson admonishes, certain of the category nodes must further be linked to representations specifying *inter alia* the kind of sensory-perceptual information that enables you to recognize instances of those categories as such:

> This definition of a concept in terms of its relations to other concepts is referred to as the *configurational meaning* of a concept. The configurational meaning of a term such as ['apple'] consists of the configurations of propositions and concepts attached to the word in the network. . . . These configurations, however, do not constitute the whole meaning of ['apple']. No number of such definitions will tell a blind person what [an apple] looks like. Part of the meaning of [such] a concept must make reference to real, sensory qualities. . . . [C]onnected to apple [sic] are primitive sensory qualities such as red, yellow, and green. These percepts contain the kind of information that our system registers when we actually see a

color such as red. In summary, then, the total meaning of [the] concept is not just the other nodes it is connected to but also [*inter alia*] the sensory . . . information connected to some of these nodes (1980, 110-111).

As is inevitable in cross-disciplinary discussions of this sort, there is much in Anderson's remarks for a philosopher to worry over;[19] but the details of his theory are unimportant in the present context. What interests me here is only that his model provides a helpful framework in which to understand how the verbal report of musical knowledge, and also the acquisition of musical knowledge from a verbal report, might be accomplished. In particular, both of these achievements demand not merely the availability, nor even the schematic representation, of a linguistic vocabulary that "parses" the world in the same way perception does. Rather, what is required is the storage of perceptual and linguistic information *together*, as in Anderson's schematic network. A psychologist might say: the schema must store percept-plus-label pairs. Intuitively speaking, in order to report that you see a red object, and likewise to acquire (recognitional) knowledge of an object's color from a verbal report that it is red, your knowledge of what red looks like must be hooked up in the right way with your knowledge of what red is called. Similarly, in order to report the C-pitches of a melody, and likewise to acquire (recognitional) knowledge of a sequence of C-pitches from a report thereof, you must have in your head a schema that associates sensory-perceptual information about how those pitches sound—that is, "the kind of information that our system registers when we actually hear" C-pitches—with linguistic information about what they are called.

The obvious candidate for the job, of course, is a C-interval schema, probably couched in a chromatic scalar format of the sort envisioned in Bharucha's network model. In addition to recovering (i.e., recognizing or type-identifying) the C-intervals of a heard melody, what the trained listener needs in order to report its C-pitches is fairly trivial— viz., short-term memory for specific C-pitches and, stored somewhere in or with his C-interval schema, a representation of how the C-pitch names are associated with the C-intervals. For example, he needs to represent the fact that there is a perfect fourth between any C-sharp and the F-sharp immediately above it, a minor third between any G-natural and the E-natural immediately below it, and so forth. Then reporting the C-pitches is simply a matter of inferring their names from their relative intervallic distances (or scale degree positions).[20] (Here I mean ordinary explicit "personal-level" inference, not the recherché sub-personal brand of Fodor's input systems.) Very roughly, following Bharucha and Anderson, it is plausible to suppose that stimulation from incoming tones activates the corresponding input nodes ("per-cepts") in the C-interval schema, which activation in turn spreads to interval category nodes (PERFECT FOURTH, MINOR THIRD, etc.) and from there to linguistic term nodes for the names of the corresponding C-pitches (and, of course, to nodes for the names of the C-intervals). (This process obviously requires short-term memory for specific pitch information in the case of melodic intervals; an interval is just the distance between two pitches, so identifying a melodic interval must require short-term memory for the first of the two.) *Vice versa*, presum-ably, for C-pitch knowledge *acquisition* by report: here activation spreads from term nodes to category nodes to percepts, thereby positioning the listener to recognize instances (performances) of the pitches in question. Since *ex hypothesi* our trained listener lacks perfect pitch, we will have to tell him the name of the first pitch, or the key signature, of the melody in question in order to "get him started" in the reporting task, and play him the first pitch to get him started in the recognition task; but those are the *only* cues he will need.

A plausible hypothesis posits similar operations with respect to the report, and knowledge acquisition by report, of the structural features of the music generally. In other words, the trained listener is likely to possess schemas of one sort or another for metrical, grouping, time-span, and prolongational structure *inter alia*, whose activation underwrites his report, and knowledge acquisition by report, of the corresponding musical features. It is not, of course, that without these enduring mental representations the listener would be wholly bereft of vocabulary in which to refer to, or even identify, the musical structures he hears. Obviously he could *refer* to a given heard C-pitch as, say, "the pitch on which Pinchas Zuckerman opened the first movement of the Brahms d minor violin sonata in his Carnegie Hall recital on November 25, 1973." This would even be an absolute identification of sorts, for he would not be comparing the pitch to any others. But it is equally obvious, I take it, that he would not thereby be identifying that C-pitch *as a token of a certain C-pitch type*—and type-identification, recognition, is what's at issue here. Such an anemic "identification" reminds us of Wittgenstein's lovely example: "Imagine someone saying: 'But I know how tall I am!' and laying his hand on top of his head to prove it" (1958, 96).

4.5 Looking Ahead

In light of these reflections, we can now pose the following question: Might it not be the case that we have conscious access to a level of mental representation of the musical signal which, unlike our recovery of the C-pitches and other deeper structures, fails to be schematized in the manner required for verbal report? In other words, might there not be a level of representation that slips through the schematic cracks, as it were, *en route* to conscious awareness?

Chapter 5

The Ineffability of Musical Nuance

Art and science are not altogether alien.

Nelson Goodman 1976, 255

5.1 Why We Cannot Report the Nuances: No Verbalization Without Schematization

I shall come straight to the point. We have hypothesized that a mapping of the N-level into a C-interval schema is a psychologically necessary condition of the trained listener's report of the C-pitches (and, of course, C-intervals) he hears in a tonal melody. (For the time being I shall set aside the matter of his knowledge *acquisition* by report; nevertheless it should be fairly clear, at each step of the way, how the acquisition story would go. The topic of acquisition will reemerge explicitly near the end of this chapter.) By parity of reasoning, we may suppose that a mapping of the N-level into schemas for *N*-intervals would be a necessary condition of the report of heard N-pitches (and N-intervals) as such. In other words, the verbal report of pitches as tokens of types more fine-grained than the chromatic types would presuppose the activation of microtonal interval schemas correspondingly more fine-grained than our C-interval ones.

And there's the rub: *it is overwhelmingly unlikely that we have, or even could have, interval schemas as fine-grained as the N-pitches and N-intervals we can hear.* Evidence from a variety of sources points to this conclusion. First are a number of psychological studies on the type-identification of musical intervals; for example, Burns and Ward (1982) report that trained listeners are not, in general, able to categorize reliably the [intervals] to a finer degree than chromatic semits [semitones—D.R.]. For example, they are not able to identify consistently quartertones between chromatic semits. . . . The inability to categorize the isolated intervals more precisely is also true of Indian musicians . . . whose scales theoretically include microtonal variations of certain intervals (249). . . . [T]he evidence indicates that the 12-interval chromatic scale may, indeed, reflect some sort of limit on the number of intervals per octave that are of practical use in music or, at least, that the semit is probably the smallest usable separation between successively played tones (247).[1]

Granted, the difficulty *could* turn out to be a mere "naming" problem— so that listeners are in fact able to type-identify (recognize, categorize) N-intervals but for some reason cannot learn names for them. But of course there is no good reason to think that is so. The interval names 'quarter-tone', 'eighth-tone', 'sixteenth-tone', and so on are no different in kind from 'whole-tone' and 'semitone', and we have no trouble applying the latter. On the contrary, the only remotely plausible explanation for our apparent inability to report the N-intervals we hear is that we lack schemas for them: we can't name them because we can't recognize them, and we can't recognize them because we can't *remember* them.

To be sure, it is entirely possible that some of us, with a great deal of practice, could acquire schemas more fine-grained than our present chromatic ones—quarter-tone schemas, say. In their 1978 categorical perception study, for example, Burns and Ward found that several subjects "were able to identify the quarter tone between M3 [major third] and P4 [perfect fourth] consistently" (460). (See also Jordan 1987 in this connection.) Nevertheless, even granting the possibility of such an enhancement of our schematic repertoire, it remains overwhelmingly unlikely that we could acquire interval schemas *as fine-grained as the pitch and interval discriminations we can make*. In the first place, if the *raison d'être* of schematization is to reduce information load, it is hard to see what point there would be to a schema whose "grain" was as fine as that of perception. Indeed, the C-interval schemas presumably serve to reduce the information load imposed precisely by the nuance representations of the N-level. Burns and Ward observe:

Numerous studies have indicated...that when faced with high information signals and/or high information rates, observers tend to encode the information into categories as a means of reducing the information load. It is probable that such factors have dictated both the use of discrete pitch relationships (rather than continuous glides and sweeps, for example) and the number of practical discrete categories. . . . [T]he use of a relatively small number of discrete pitch relationships in music is probably dictated by inherent limitations on the processing of high information-load stimuli by human sensory systems (1982, 245, 264).

Second, the just noticeable difference (JND) for pitch is known to vary with the frequency, intensity, length, and waveform of the tones heard, as well as with the age, alertness, and health of the listener, among other factors (cf., e.g., Seashore 1967, 59–62); a similar variability undoubtedly attends the interval JND as well. In view of such inconstancies, it is very hard to see how a listener could establish long-term mental structures of the sort at issue.

Perhaps the strongest testimony to our lack of N-interval schemas, however, is the fact that we hear out-of-tune intervals as precisely that—out-of-tune. The point is, an interval is out-of-tune only relative to some standard or prototype—here, only relative to the correct width of some C-interval; we hear mistuned intervals as mistuned instances of the twelve C-intervals, not as in-tune instances of microtonal N-intervals. Indeed, it may well be that, if N-interval schemas commensurate with our pitch and interval discriminations were activated in music perception, we would never hear *any* interval (or pitch or chord) as being out-of-tune. And that brings me to a philosophically important point. We have heard that musical schemas underwrite the listener's apprehension of the structure of a tonal work; for instance, it is apparently the imposition of C-interval schemas (among others) that sifts a tonal melody out from the teeming profusion of nuances recovered in the N-level. Our schemas determine which pitch differences get noticed and which get ignored, they make acoustically identical events sound different and acoustically different ones sound identical, all depending upon the pushes and pulls of the current tonal context. Accordingly: change the schemas and, in all probability, you change the way the music sounds. In particular, it is plausible to suppose that if N-interval schemas were activated in the perception of a musical performance, every nuance therein—every determinate pitch and interval we can hear—would be *recognized*, and the melody (for one) would vanish in a sea of fine details.[2] In such a circumstance, I want to say, we would not be hearing the music *as tonal*: tonal music just is music whose melodies and harmonies soar out from the background welter.

In sum, it appears that we do not have, nor are we likely to acquire, nor—insofar as I'm right about the transfiguring effects of N-interval schemas on perception—could we mobilize in the perception of tonal music *as such* even if we did have, interval schemas as fine-grained as the nuances we can hear. On the view propounded here, it follows that we will be unable to type-identify, hence unable to report, the N-pitches and N-intervals represented in the N-level. This is not to suggest, of course, that the nuances are somehow incoherent or "meaningless." As I have repeatedly noted, the performer's objective is to mold these fine-grained features in such a way as to communicate his hearing of a work's structure; and in so doing he can surely play, and *mean* to play, his leading tones high and his vibrato wide. But the point is that none of this reflects a mental categorization or type-identification of nuances as such: for all intents and purposes, 'high' and 'wide' are as fine-grained as you are going to get in the way of "identifications" at this shallow level.

It is tempting to stop here and conclude that our conscious knowledge of musical nuances is (nuance) ineffable: lacking sufficiently fine-grained interval schemas—that is, lacking sufficiently fine-grained interval *memory*—we cannot type-identify, hence cannot report, the N-pitches and N-intervals we consciously hear in a musical signal. And indeed that *is* where I shall end up, but only after smoothing out a remaining wrinkle.

5.2 Do We Know What We Cannot Say?

Recall that our goal is to provide a psychologically respectable account of ineffable musical *knowledge*—that is, something we consciously know but cannot report or communicate in words. I have suggested that we can't report the N-pitches (and N-intervals) we hear because we can't type-identify them by ear, and we can't type-identify them because we lack the appropriate schemas. But then, you may reasonably object, by the same token we don't *know* what their types are, either; to know what their types are, in the perceptual sense at issue, would just *be* to type-identify them. And if we don't know what their types are, then there is an important sense in which we don't know which N-pitch or N-interval we are hearing at any given moment. If that is so, then what is it that we know but cannot say? In other words, what do we know ineffably?[3]

Grasping the answer here requires seeing things in just the right way. Consider again the type-identification of C-pitches (taken as exemplifying the structural features generally). What do you, as trained listener, know in that case? A first reply might be: of any acoustic event you hear in a performance, you know (by ear) which C-pitch type it is a token of. However, your knowledge of the C-pitches also admits of a second, somewhat thinner characterization, viz.: of any acoustic event you hear in a performance, you know *how it sounds*. (The fudge is deliberate but short-lived, I promise.) What then do you accomplish in reporting your knowledge of the C-pitches? How is success measured here? A first reply might be: your knowledge report succeeds to the extent that, solely in virtue of hearing that report, another trained listener can recognize subsequent instantiations (performances) of those C-pitches as such. However, the success of your knowledge report also admits of a second, somewhat thinner characterization, viz.: your knowledge report succeeds to the extent that, solely in virtue of hearing that report, another trained listener comes to know what you know— which is: *how those C-pitches sound*. To frame the point in cognitivist terms, your knowledge report succeeds to the extent that it brings about a reproduction of the relevant sensory-perceptual (here, C-pitch) representations in the mind of one who hears and understands it. (Recall the discussion of musical communication in §3.6.) When you successfully report to another trained listener the C-pitches of a piece you have heard, there is formed in his mind-brain a sensory-perceptual representation of those pitches—i.e., a representation of how they sound or "feel"—that is more or less identical to the one in your mind-brain.

I have belabored the foregoing points because understanding them is essential to understanding how our knowledge of the N-pitches and N-intervals in a performance differs from our knowledge of the C-pitches and C-intervals, and, in particular, what it is that we know but cannot say in the former case. Surely in hearing the nuances you are acquiring knowledge of them *at least* in the "thin" sense invoked above: you have a sensory-perceptual mental representation of them, *you know how they sound.* It may be objected that whereas you know how the acoustic events of the performance sound *qua C-pitches,* you precisely do *not* know how they sound *qua nuances;* and that that difference makes all the difference where claims of knowledge are concerned. This complaint smudges an important distinction, however; for although it is true that you don't know how the events of the performance sound *qua tokens of particular nuance types,* you certainly do know how they sound *qua* nuances as opposed to, say, *qua* C-pitches. In other words, you hear them as nuances, and therein know that they are nuances (as opposed to, say, C-pitches); it's just that, for lack of interval schemas sufficiently fine-grained to permit type-identifications, you don't know *which* nuances they are. Hence although in hearing the nuances you know how they sound, there will be nothing you can say, no report you can make, that could by itself serve to reproduce that knowledge in the mind-brain of another listener. On the contrary, your only hope of getting him to know what you know is to *ostend* the signal; he must hear it for himself. To put the point another way: you must *show* him, you cannot *tell* him, what you know. Do not misunderstand: certainly we could coin (type-identifying) names for the N-pitches—names like, say, 'A-natural(1)', 'A-natural(12)', 'B-flat(10)', and so forth—just as we could coin names for all the determinate shades we can see. But for want of the requisite schemas in long-term memory, we would not be able to apply those names "by ear." In this respect the nuances are known ineffably—are, as I shall say, *nuance ineffable.*

Two points of clarification. First, I said that ostension is your only *hope* for communication. In point of fact, even ostension typically will not suffice, since any two listeners are bound to differ somewhere in their discrimination profiles; in virtue of brute hardware disparities, they will hear different N-pitches and N-intervals in the same acoustic signal. As a result, ostension guarantees communication only among listeners whose discrimination profiles are identical under all relevant listening conditions. For ease of discussion, however, I shall suppose that the discrimination profiles of different trained listeners are identical; doing so poses no threat to my view, since such disparities only render our knowledge of musical nuances the more ineffable. Second, it may be objected that one could report one's knowledge of the nuances by making comparative ("same/different"), rather than so-called absolute, identifications; that is, that one could effectively type-identify (and hence report) heard N-pitches and N-intervals by matching them to presented N-pitch and N-interval standards, much as one might identify the shades of colored objects by matching them to standard chips in a color chart. The difficulty here is that matchings of the sort envisioned, even if they did amount to type-identifications, would just *be* identifications by ostension: matching a heard N-pitch (or N-interval) to a presented standard would just *be* an identifying of one pitch (or interval) *by pointing to* another. Thus the nuances would remain ineffable.

There will be those who insist that knowledge is by its nature both enduring and verbally expressible, hence that our representations of musical nuances do not properly speaking count as *knowledge* of them. And perhaps that is, in the end, the right thing to say. Nevertheless, I ask such objectors to keep in mind the following pair of considerations. First, if the N-level does not count as knowledge of the pitch and interval nuances, then so far as I can see, *nothing* does. That is to say, if the N-level is not knowledge, then there is *no such thing* as knowledge (or human knowledge, anyway) of the determinate pitch of a tone or the determinate width of an interval. (What else could play the part? Perhaps it will be said that knowing the determinate pitch of a tone just consists in being able to match it to a presented standard in the manner described above; but even on such an "ability" construal, the knowledge in question is ephemeral or nonenduring: given our lack of nuance schemas, you would be able to perform the matching only so long as you were actually occurrently *hearing* the nuance in question.) By the same token, insofar as our schemas for color suffer limitations analogous to those suffered by our interval schemas (cf., e.g., Hardin 1988), there will be no knowing the determinate shades of the objects we see; and similarly, *mutatis mutandis*, in respect of numerous other sensory-perceptual properties. I shall not pursue the issue here—obviously a great deal more would need to be said; let me simply point out that such consequences might be thought a high price to pay for any conception of knowledge that yields them. Don't I know the determinate pitch of a tone when I am listening to it? or the determinate shade of an object when I am looking at it?

Second, as I said at the outset, my goal here is to discover elements of real-time musical experience that might account for the claims of ineffable knowledge so often registered in the philosophical literature. (An exercise in the psychology of philosophy, if you will.) At the moment I am proposing that our conscious perception of musical nuances is a likely candidate. Hence although I find it plausible to regard the N-level as an instance of musical *knowledge,* and have lately gestured toward some of the reasons why, the success of my project here does not depend on this; in other words, the success of my project does not require that the N-level *be* an instance of knowledge. I shall continue to speak of it as such, however, pending further discussion at another time and place.

The foregoing argument from the nuances may seem to have turned a firebird to a pullet—a rich, profound, even mystical feature of musical experience to desiccated scientific fact. (Artists are always worried about what they envision as the rape of aesthetic experience at the heavy hands of psychologists.) I suppose there might be something to this indictment were I claiming that the case of the pitch and interval nuances tells the whole story about the nuance ineffability—*a fortiori* about musical ineffability generally. However, as I noted early on, I conceive the N-pitches and N-intervals as just two among a constellation of nuance features, each engendering a similar speechlessness. There is every reason to suppose that musical performances sustain fine details of duration, loudness, speed, articulation, and timbre, among others; for example, the nuance ineffability of keyboard and percussion performances, like their "expressiveness" itself, presumably derives more from their nuances of duration, loudness, and speed than from any N-pitches or N-intervals. Indeed, nuances of speed and timing may be the performer's preeminent communicative tool (see, e.g., Drake and Palmer 1991, Gabrielsson 1986, and Jones 1990a for highly suggestive data).[4]

Resorting to the vague and sentimental terminology I have till now sought to abandon, I am imagining the stream of nuance pitches, intervals, durations, speeds, dynamics, and the rest as a kind of evanescent corona shimmering around the structural frame of the piece. The question is whether this corona engenders an aesthetically significant kind of ineffability. Arguments presented here are obviously intended to inspire an affirmative answer, but however the question is ultimately decided, we have in posing it reached a border where psychology ends and philosophy begins. Home at last.

5.3 Cavell Revisited

I have touted my cognitivist account as a psychological complement to some of the traditional philosophical writings on musical ineffability. Let us turn again to Cavell's "Music Discomposed" (1976) as a testing ground; if things go well, the meeting will foster a reciprocal sharpening of views. The "relaxed" character of our appeal to Cavell should be kept in mind throughout, however; I use his remarks more as a foil for my own story than anything else, and I shall not here be giving his discussion the careful examination it deserves.

Thus far I have taken Cavell's "knowledge in sensing" or "in feeling" to be, simply, sensory-perceptual or felt knowledge ('knowledge$_{sp}$'). And certainly he does mean to claim, at a minimum, that knowledge of musical works is knowledge of this kind. However, I have also hinted at a stronger reading of Cavell's words—one according to which musical knowledge is an *occurrent* phenomenon, so that musical works are known only *while being* perceived or felt. The following passages are suggestive in this regard:

> Why does the assertion "You have to *hear* it!" mean what it does?. . . . Perhaps the question is: How does it happen that the *achievement* or *result* of using a sense organ comes to be thought of as the *activity* of that organ—as though the aesthetic experience had the form not merely of a continuous effort (e.g., listening) but of a continuous achievement . . . (78).

> [I] find that I can't *tell* you. I want to tell you because the knowledge, unshared, is a burden. . . . [U]nless I can tell what I know, there is a suggestion . . . that I do *not* know. But I *do*—what I [hear] is *that* (pointing to the object). But for that to communicate, you have to

[hear] it too (193). . . . [W]orks of art are objects of the sort that can only be *known in sensing* (80).

Cavell's point, I take it, is that only reference *by ostension* can serve to communicate my knowledge of a piece of music (or other artwork). 'Only' is important here. It is not merely that ostension is required *at some point*—say, in the learning of relevant terminology (like interval and chord names). Rather, the claim seems to be that ostension is *always* required for the communication of musical knowledge; such knowledge can *never* be conveyed by language. Instead, I must always show you, always acquaint you with, what I hear.

Now if ostension is always required for the communication of a certain kind of knowledge, then that knowledge must be *essentially* occurrent in nature; that is, it must be a kind of knowledge that cannot be retained. (Contrapositively: if we could retain it, then we wouldn't need the ostension in order to communicate it. For example, because you can remember what scarlet looks like, and of course what it is called, I need not ostend an instance of scarlet in order to communicate to you the knowledge that a given object has that color.) But if we cannot retain the knowledge in question, then we cannot learn words by which to communicate it (in the recognitional sense of 'communicate' here at issue). To that extent, such knowledge is ineffable: for you to know what I know of the music, you must perceive it—nay, *be perceiving* it—yourself.

Cavell writes:

> It is not, as in the case of ordinary material objects, that I know *because* I see, or that seeing is *how* I know (as opposed, for example, to being told, or figuring it out). It is rather...that *what* I know is what I see; or even: seeing feels like knowing. ("Seeing the point" conveys this sense, but in ordinary cases of seeing the point, once it's seen it's known, or understood; about works of art one may wish to say that they require a continuous seeing of the point.) (78–79)

In other words, in the musical case, it's not that I know merely *by* hearing (as opposed to, say, by being told). 'Knowing by hearing' seems to suggest that the hearing can be merely instrumental, that the knowledge is an end product independent of the causative sense perception.

Not surprisingly, this independence is plausibly conceived in terms of post-perceptual retention or endurance. Such a view allows that knowledge by or because of hearing could be either mere "propositional" or "descriptive" knowledge (call it 'knowledge$_d$'), on the one hand, or enduring sensory-perceptual knowledge "contingently" acquired by hearing (e.g., knowledge$_{sp}$ of the C-pitches of a tonal melody, which could also be acquired by description), on the other. In the passages cited above, Cavell explicitly repudiates knowledge *by hearing* as a candidate for knowledge of an artwork. In its stead? '*What* I know is what I hear' must mean not simply 'I know the work *by* hearing it', but rather 'Knowing the work *is* hearing it', or, better, 'What I know is what I *am hearing*'. Cavell's use of the preposition 'in' with the gerundive (as in 'known in sensing') only reinforces a picture of artistic knowledge as an occurrent activity or process.

The kinship with our cognitivist notion of nuance ineffability is clear. On Cavell's view and ours alike, the ineffable musical knowledge turns out to be knowledge communicable, if at all, only by ostension; and ostension is required because the only way to know the music is to *be hearing* it.[5] Like most kinships, however, this one is not without its frictions. As we have just seen, to say (as Cavell does) that musical artworks can *only* be known in sensing or feeling (or as I would rather put it: can be known *only* in sensing or feeling) is not merely to say that knowledge of musical artworks is sensory-perceptual or "felt" knowledge; on the contrary, it is minimally to rule out knowledge$_{sp}$ that can be acquired by description. But then it seems to follow that our knowledge$_{sp}$ of musical structure, as opposed to our knowledge$_{sp}$ of the nuances, fails to count as knowledge of a musical *work*. And that just cannot be right: on any view, cognitivist or otherwise, our knowledge$_{sp}$ of musical structure is the best candidate we have for knowledge of a piece of music. How are we to make sense of Cavell's claim here?

The answer is already in hand. On the cognitivist view I have defended, it is our knowledge$_{sp}$ of musical *nuances*—as opposed to musical structures—that is communicable solely by ostension. And these fine-grained details, recall, are features of particular *performances* of a work; as I have emphasized, the nuances are what vary from performance to performance, *ipso facto* serving to distinguish one performance from another, while the structural features remain more or less constant. (Their instantiation of the relevant structural features is, after all, what makes performances performances *of a given work*; see again §2.4.) Thus on my view it is performances of musical works, rather than the works themselves, that are knowable *only in sensing* or *in feeling*. Our knowledge of works and performances alike is sensory-perceptual or felt knowledge, but only performances need be *perceived* to be known. What I want to suggest, then, is that an "occurrent" reading of Cavell's remarks applies similarly to performances rather than works. I suspect there is no coincidence in the fact that his only illustration of ineffable musical knowledge pertains to performances: "You don't know what I mean when I say that Schnabel's slow movements give the impression of infinite length" (79).[6]

Perhaps the idea that knowledge of an artwork requires or even consists in sense perception of it[7] is born of a bias toward the visual arts. Naturally I can acquire some knowledge$_{sp}$ of, say, Picasso's *The Old Guitarist* by being told its colors, shapes, textures and so forth, just as I acquire some knowledge$_{sp}$ of a man's appearance when you tell me he is wearing his blue serge suit. But surely I do not therein come to know the work *in its entirety*. In seeing the painting, in being visually acquainted with it, I acquire knowledge of it that I could not have acquired otherwise: at the very least, my knowledge$_{sp}$ by seeing is considerably more precise (we might say: more determinate) than my knowledge$_{sp}$ by description, because the perception contains information too fine-grained to secure lodging in long-term memory. So there is an important sense in which I do need to be perceptually acquainted with a visual work in order to know it. But consider the literary work. With what must I be perceptually acquainted in order to know Austen's *Pride and Prejudice?* Ink marks on paper? Raised dots? Oscillating air molecules? One of these, perhaps, but no *particular* one.

The obvious difference, you may object, is that knowledge of a visual work is knowledge$_{sp}$, whereas knowledge of a linguistic work is knowledge$_d$; it is hardly surprising, therefore, that my knowledge by description of the Austen should be superior to my knowledge by description of the Picasso. However, at least two considerations serve to quash this objection. First, perhaps knowing *Pride and Prejudice* does require knowing$_{sp}$ how its words sound (this would be all the more true of poetic works, I imagine), but that hardly requires sensory-perceptual confrontation with an utterance of them; I know what English sounds like, I don't need to hear it spoken any more. To put the point another way, I am not suggesting that no knowledge$_{sp}$ is required for knowledge of *Pride and Prejudice,* but rather no *sense perception* of it. Second, consider the place of musical works in this scenario. I have claimed that in principle the trained listener can acquire knowledge$_{sp}$ of musical structures—that is, recognitional sensory-perceptual knowledge—simply by being told what they are (cf. §3.2); and if, as we have been supposing, a piece of music is to be identified at least in part with such structures, then my claim amounts to saying that the trained listener can acquire knowledge$_{sp}$ of a piece of music by description. What this shows, I think, is that the critical difference between paintings on the one hand, and novels and musical works on the other, is not the difference between knowledge$_{sp}$ and knowledge$_d$, but rather the difference between having a "schematizable" structure and lacking one: it is the presence of such (apprehendable) structure in musical and linguistic works that enables us to acquire knowledge of them independently of any sensory-perceptual acquaintance with their material (acoustic, plastic) instantiations. One might say that, because music and language are thus structured, knowledge by description of string quartets and novels can be exhaustive in a way that knowledge by description of a painting, or of the gentleman's blue serge suit, or of a *performance* of a string quartet, cannot.[8]

Of course such a claim, even if plausible, is plausible only as far as it goes: it applies only to pieces of music that sustain such a structure. What about a work like John Cage's 4'33"? Is it knowable, exhaustively, by description? We cannot afford to explore this familiar morass here, but its appearance suggests that such philosophical chestnuts as 'What, or where, is the piece of music?' are likely to find hybrid answers— answers that are partly conceptual and partly empirical, part philosophy and part psychology. That, I think, is a moral of this meeting of aesthetics and cognitive theory.

5.4 Why Do We Notice What We Cannot Say?

As with respect to the feeling ineffability, I owe some explanation for our *attention* to the nuance ineffability in our musical knowledge$_{sp}$. After all, our knowledge$_{sp}$ of the many determinate shades and shapes and tastes and textures of everyday life is bound to be similarly ineffable, yet we feel no special compulsion to communicate it. Inasmuch as they are recovered at shallow processing levels, the nuances are plausibly regarded as features of the "surface" of a performance; and the idea that aesthetic experience is characterized by attention to the sensed surfaces of things is hardly new.[9] What one wants to understand, though, in the musical case in particular, is *why* our attention is thus directed, and whence the urge to verbalize.

In chapter 3 (§3.2) I observed that art is standardly conceived as a form of expression; and I speculated that, since language is our expressive paradigm, and since music (more so than the other nonlinguistic arts) is kin to language in certain important respects, an expressivist conception might account in part for the impulse to *tell* what we know of a musical work. At this juncture I want to urge that the same should be said of performances. If the piece is the composer's expression, the performance is the performer's, and "the first fact" about performances, as well as pieces, is that they are *meant*: the performer *means* to play this E-natural ever so slightly high, to sustain that leading tone a hair too long, to stress the downbeats a tad more than the upbeats, in order to communicate his proprietary hearing of the structure of a piece. Conceived in this way, the performance is itself a work of art with its own robust brand of ineffable knowledge.

I have also suggested (cf. §2.5) that intrasubjective variations in the structural descriptions of a given work over repeated hearings might partially account for our persistent interest in live performance. The foregoing characterization of our knowledge$_{sp}$ of musical nuances may contribute a further piece of the puzzle: perhaps it is the fleeting character of that knowledge$_{sp}$—the fact that we cannot *remember* the nuances of a performance with any precision—that keeps us ever coming back for more: the only way to know a performance is to *be hearing* it. Whereas you can remember, and hence know in advance, how a given piece will go, a performance—even a performance you have heard repeatedly on tape—promises the thrill of the unexpected: you never know exactly what you will hear.[10]

Before we stop, it is worth remarking that the need to advert to more "traditional" terminology (e.g., my talk of the performance nuances as "an evanescent corona shimmering around the structural frame of the piece") can hardly be incidental. Rather, it reinforces the conviction that we need both ways of talking about artistic experience—the more introspective and metaphorical vocabulary of traditional aesthetics, and the more empirical, and to that extent more "literal," vocabulary of contemporary cognitive theory. Jerry Fodor suggests that, for philosophers like Dewey and Austin, "philosophy is what you do to a problem until it becomes clear enough to solve it by doing science" (1981a, 177). Our progress here suggests a reverse course: that science is what you do to a problem until it becomes, for want of a better term, problematical enough to solve it by doing philosophy.[11]

Chapter 6

Naturalizing Nelson Goodman

The moral is, I think, that we ought to stop asking for analyses; cognitive psychology is all the philosophy of mind we are likely to get.

Jerry Fodor 1981a, 202

In preceding chapters I have made the case for an accord between my cognitivist theory of musical ineffability and some of Stanley Cavell's remarks on the subject. That endeavor demanded a (shall we say) "creative" handling of the Cavell text, and, though I find the results plausible, others may find them forced. With Nelson Goodman's *Languages of Art*,[1] on the other hand, the situation is altogether different. Here we find a strikingly clear case of philosophy "rediscovered and vindicated by cognitive science." Although we shall discover that Goodman's account of musical ineffability may be untenable as it stands, our cognitivist theory so closely parallels his that it reclaims about as much as one could reasonably hope for. In particular, our third species of ineffability, the nuance ineffability, is an almost perfect realization of what Goodman has in mind.

Chapter 6 has four parts. *Part One* presents Goodman's analysis of musical ineffability. Since his position is made explicit only with respect to the nature of artistic ineffability generally, we must glean his specific account of the musical kind as it follows therefrom; it follows directly, however. *Part Two* then marks the spot where Goodman's theory and our cognitivist one cross paths. *Part Three* exposes a potential problem for Goodman's view; and then *Part Four* shows that, whatever the final verdict on Goodman's analysis as it stands, his central insight finds safe harbor in our theory in a "psychologized" form. Because *Languages of Art* invokes a good deal of semiotic technique, the going will be a bit

woolly at times; as throughout, however, I shall do my best to introduce
only such machinery as the succeeding discussion demands.

6.1 Part One: The Analysis

According to Goodman, artworks and their scores, scripts, diagrams,
blueprints, sketches, and performances alike are *symbols*, and they
instantiate virtually every symbolic relation under the sun: they denote,
refer, represent, notate, exemplify, express, describe. We shall be concerned primarily with his theory of musical symbolism, but an understanding of the latter requires some familiarity with certain general
features of his approach. It is best to begin by acquainting ourselves
with seven of the parameters (three syntactic and four semantic) in
respect of which Goodman distinguishes "the varied systems of sym-
bolization used in art, science, and life in general."

The seven are as follows:

(1) *Syntactic disjointness.* A syntactically disjoint symbol
     scheme is one in which no syntactic token ("mark" or
     "marking") belongs to more than one syntactic type
     ("character").[2]

For example, a scheme consisting of the reduced Arabic fractional
numerals (call this 'scheme A') and a scheme consisting of vertical lines
ordered according to their lengths in fractions of an inch (call this
'scheme B') are both syntactically disjoint. By contrast, a scheme in
which one character consists of vertical lines between 1 and 3 inches
long, and another character consists of vertical lines between 1 and 2
inches long, is not (130–135).

(2) *Semantic disjointness.* A semantically disjoint symbol
     system is one in which no two characters have any mem-
     ber of their respective extensions ("compliance-classes") in
     common.[3]

Both schemes A and B, taking as compliants (say) "physical objects
according to their weights in fractions of an ounce" (153), are semantically disjoint. By contrast, the English language, which contains both
'doctor' and 'Englishman', is not (152).

(3)   *Syntactic differentiation.* A syntactically differentiated symbol scheme is one such that, for any two distinct characters and any token mark that does not belong to both, it is theoretically possible[4] to determine of at least one of the characters that the mark does not belong to it.

Here A and B diverge, says Goodman: A is syntactically differentiated, but B is not: in B there will be some two (indeed, infinitely many) characters L and L', and some line *l* that does not belong to both, such that it is impossible to determine of either character that *l* fails to belong to it; in other words, it is impossible to determine that the length of *l* is nonidentical either to (the length specified by) L or to (the length specified by) L' (137). (If you suspect something is amiss with [3], and also with [4] below, you are right; more on that momentarily.)

(4)   *Semantic differentiation.* A semantically differentiated symbol system is one such that, for any two characters with distinct compliance-classes, and any object that does not in fact comply with both characters, it is theoretically possible to determine of at least one of the characters that the object does not comply with it.

Neither A nor B (as interpreted in [2] above) is semantically differentiated, Goodman tells us: in both cases, there will be two (indeed, infinitely many) characters with distinct compliance-classes, and some object that does not comply with both, such that in principle it cannot be determined, of either character, that the object fails to comply with it. By contrast, a system consisting of the fully reduced Arabic fractional numerals, taking as compliants the fully reduced Arabic fractional numerals, is semantically differentiated.

(5)   *Ambiguity.* An ambiguous symbol system is one in which some characters have more than one compliance-class.

English, which contains words like 'bow' and 'bank', is of course ambiguous; A and B are not.

(6)   *Syntactic density.* A syntactically dense symbol scheme is one that "provides for infinitely many characters so ordered that between any two there is a third" (136).

Both A and B are syntactically dense; the English alphabet, on the other hand, is not. Of course the important difference between A and B is that, in the latter scheme but not in the former, there is between any two characters a third *less discriminable from each of them than they are from each other* (1976, 136); hence B, but not A, is syntactically undifferentiated. When Goodman says 'dense' he often means 'dense and undifferentiated', but I shall generally avoid that abbreviation since it tends to obscure some important distinctions.

> (7)   *Semantic density.* A semantically dense symbol system is one that provides for infinitely many compliance-classes so ordered that between any two there is a third.

Both A and B are semantically dense, whereas the English alphabet, taking as compliants (say) the first 26 U.S. presidents, is not.

Now before we proceed further, a modification of the above definitions is in order. In particular, (3) and (4), the definitions of differentiation, do not capture what must (or at least *should*) be Goodman's intent. For example, scheme B is supposed to be syntactically undifferentiated. On (3) as it stands, this means there will be some two characters *L* and *L'*, and some line *l* that does not belong to both, such that it is not theoretically possible to *determine* of either *L* or *L'* that *l* does not belong to it. But this will not do: if *l* differs in length from (the length specified by) either *L* or *L'* or both, it so differs *at some finite point*. Hence it will always be theoretically possible to build a measuring device sufficiently fine-grained to register the difference. If scheme B is to count as undifferentiated, (3) must be strengthened. I propose the following:

> (3')   *Syntactic differentiation.* A syntactically differentiated scheme is one such that, for any character *C* and any mark *m*, it is theoretically possible to determine either that *m* belongs to *C* or that *m* does not belong to *C*.

On the simplifying assumption that every mark belongs to one and only one character, we get the result that, for any mark m, it is theoretically possible to determine which character m belongs to. (I shall make this assumption throughout; nothing essential to my position depends on it.) In somewhat more intuitive terms, a syntactically differentiated scheme is one in which it is theoretically possible to uniquely type-identify any mark. Then with regard to scheme B, although we will be able to determine, of any character to which a given line does not belong, that the line does not belong to it, we will not be able to determine which character the line *does* belong to. An analogous adjustment should be made in the semantic case:

(4') *Semantic differentiation.* A semantically differentiated symbol system is one such that, for any character C and any object o, it is theoretically possible to determine either that o complies with C or that o does not comply with C.

On the assumption that every object complies with one and only one character, we get the result that, for any object o, it is theoretically possible to determine which character o complies with (i.e., which compliance-class it is in).[5]

That these recastings of (3) and (4) capture Goodman's true intent is evident in passages like the following:

Suppose we have a simple pressure gauge with a circular face and a single pointer that moves smoothly clockwise as the pressure increases. If there are no figures or other marks on the face, and every difference in pointer position constitutes a difference in character, the...requirement of syntactic differentiation is not met; for we can never *determine the position of the pointer with absolute precision.* And since the semantic ordering—of pressures—is also dense, semantic as well as syntactic differentiation is lacking (157; my emphasis).

The more delicate and precise the stipulated differentiation between characters . . ., the harder it will be to determine whether certain marks belong to one character or another (134). . . . [In an undifferentiated scheme,] no mark can be determined to belong to one rather than to many other characters (136).

From now on, when I speak of differentiation I shall have (3') and (4') in mind.

Armed with the foregoing definitions, Goodman turns out a detailed analysis of the various symbolic relations effective in the arts. For instance, pictorial representation is (among other things) denotation in a syntactically and semantically dense and undifferentiated system (e.g., painted marks on canvas); literary expression is metaphorical exemplification in a syntactically disjoint and differentiated but semantically dense, undifferentiated, and ambiguous system (viz. the natural language); musical notation is denotation in a syntactically and semantically disjoint and differentiated, unambiguous system (viz. the score). Most important for our purposes, though, is the resulting characterization of artistic ineffability:

> Impossibility of finite determination [viz. undifferentiatedness—
> D.R.] may carry some suggestion of the ineffability so often claimed
> for, or charged against, the aesthetic. But density, far from mysterious and vague, is explicitly defined; it arises out of, and sustains,
> the unsatisfiable demand for absolute precision. . . . [I]neffability
> upon analysis turns into density rather than mystery (253).

(In the above, 'dense' means 'dense and undifferentiated'.) Very roughly, Goodman's thought seems to be that our knowledge of artworks is ineffable insofar as we cannot determine—*a fortiori* cannot say—precisely what their syntactic features are (e.g., their precise colors, shapes, pitches, durations), nor precisely what they symbolize. In other words, our knowledge of artworks is ineffable insofar as they are (syntactically and/or semantically) dense and undifferentiated. I shall leave it at that, for now; things will come more clearly into focus once we have had a look at some musical examples.

As Goodman sees it, there are two primary symbols in music: the score and the performance. Between them they sustain three ineffabilities—one attending certain markings in the score, two attending certain properties of the performance. Let us consider them in that order.

6.1.1 The Score as Symbol
On Goodman's view, the musical score *denotes* those performances that *comply* with it. (He also says that the score *prescribes*, and that it *specifies*, the events of a performance. For present purposes I shall use these terms more or less interchangeably.) A performance is an acoustic object (a "sound-event") that can be "taken" in two ways, corresponding to its compliance with two kinds of musical markings: on the one hand it can be "taken as an instance of a work," and on the other hand "as a

sound-event" (237–238, e.g.). Taken in the first way, the performance complies with the notational markings in the score; taken in the second, it complies with "supplementary instructions, either printed along with the score or tacitly given by tradition, word-of-mouth, etc." (237). Let me explain the distinction.

For Goodman, 'score' is a term of art referring exclusively to those markings that denote (what he takes to be) the definitive features of a musical work—essentially, its C-pitches and its rhythms and meters:[6]

> A score, whether or not ever used as a guide for a performance, has as a primary function the authoritative identification of a work from performance to performance (128). . . . The function of a score is to specify the essential properties a performance must have to belong to the work (195). . . . .[A] musical score . . . defines a work (210).

With a handful of minor exceptions, we are told, the markings in the score constitute a *notational* system.[7] That is to say, they are (1) syntactically disjoint: for example, every token notehead is either an A-natural marking or a B-flat marking or a C-sharp marking, etc., and not more than one; (2) semantically disjoint: for example, every token sound-event complies with either the A-natural marking or the B-flat marking or the C-sharp marking, etc., and not more than one; (3) syntactically differentiated: for example, it is theoretically possible to uniquely determine which C-pitch character any token notehead belongs to; (4) semantically differentiated: for example, it is theoretically possible to uniquely determine which C-pitch character any token sound-event complies with; and (5) unambiguous: for example, no C-pitch character has more than one compliance-class. For clarity I shall refer to the notational markings as the 'Score', taking the liberty of using the uppercase letter in relevant places in citations from *Languages of Art*; by 'score' I shall mean the score in the ordinary sense of the term, as including all musical markings on the printed page, notational or otherwise. Goodman's claim is that the performance-taken-as-an-instance-of-a-work (call it the 'performance(W)') complies with the notational markings in the Score. In somewhat more intuitive terms, the performance(W) is the performance considered as an instantiation of the sequence of pitch-time events prescribed in the Score.

Now as Goodman himself points out, the "Score need not—indeed cannot—specify all aspects of the compliants nor even every degree of difference in any aspect" (195). In addition to the Scored (notational) markings, there are what he terms "supplementary instructions, either printed along with the score or tacitly given by tradition, word-of-mouth, etc." (237). These latter evidently include printed verbal directions for tempo, mood, dynamics, and articulation (e.g., 'Fast', 'Adagio', 'Mournful', 'Forte', 'Legato'), graphic indicators of dynamic level and articulation (e.g., "hairpin" *crescendo* and *decrescendo* markings, accent marks, *staccato* marks), and such informal oral injunctions as "Take more time at the cadence," "That A-natural needs to be slightly higher," and so forth. The nonnotational character of the supplementary instructions derives from several sources; just for example, hairpin dynamic markings are presumably syntactically dense and undifferentiated, while words like 'Fast', 'Forte', and 'Legato' are semantically nondisjoint.

Central to our investigation of musical ineffability, however, are the supposed *semantic density* and *undifferentiatedness* of the supplementary instructions: according to Goodman, each scheme of such instructions "provides for an infinite number of characters with compliance-classes so ordered that between each two there is a third" less discriminable from each of them than they are from each other (153). Hence there is no even theoretical possibility of saying which supplementary character any given sound-event complies with.[8] For example, "since a tempo may be prescribed as fast, or as slow, or as between fast and slow, or as between fast and between-fast-and-slow, and so on without limit, semantic differentiation goes by the board" (184–185). Similarly, one supposes, a pitch may be prescribed as a "good" A-natural, or as a slightly high A-natural, or as between a good A-natural and a slightly high A-natural, or as between a good A-natural and between-a-good-A-natural-and-a-slightly-high-A-natural, and so on without limit; a dynamic level may be prescribed as loud, or as medium loud, or as between loud and medium loud, or as between loud and between-loud-and- medium-loud, and so on without limit; etc. According to Goodman, in no such case will it be theoretically possible to determine which character any sound-event in a performance complies with; in more familiar terms, there will be no even theoretical possibility of identifying the sound-events of a performance as tokens of "supplementary" tempo or pitch or dynamic types. Note that such a result obtains independently of the vagueness of expressions like 'fast' and 'slightly high'; in other words, the supplementary instructions would be semantically undifferentiated even if they were *not* vague. For example, even (relatively) nonvague supplementary pitch names following the rational numbers—e.g., 'A-natural(1)', 'B-flat(17)', 'C-sharp(2.6)', and so forth—or any other nonvague names you like, would be semantically dense and undifferentiated.

Goodman says the following about sketches, but the same can be said of any dense and undifferentiated system:

> [N]o magnitude of difference in any respect is set as the threshold of significance. Differences of all kinds and degrees, measurable or not, are on equal footing (193).

Intuitively speaking, then, only the supplementary instructions, and not the notational (Scored) markings, can designate values that differ in degree but not in category or kind. The Score can specify an A-natural, but no particular determinate A-natural; it can specify a quarter note, but not a note of *this* particular determinate duration as opposed to *that*. Rather, these fine-grained values are specified by the supplementary instructions for performance. In the terminology of preceding chapters: the supplementary instructions specify values *within* the categories specified by the notational markings in the Score. (Of course, since the supplementary instructions are semantically undifferentiated, there will be no *determining* which within-category values they specify. See note 12.)

Now Goodman claims that the compliant of the supplementary instructions is the performance considered under its second aspect—that is, the performance taken as a sound-event (call it the 'performance(SE)'). And therein he makes a critical error. Admittedly, in one sense the claim that the supplementary instructions take the performance(SE) as their compliant is trivially true. I say 'trivially' because the claim is true with respect to *all* of the musical markings, not just the supplementary ones; it is sound-events that comply with the notational markings in the Score, too, as the following passage attests:

> If we consider piano scores alone, the language is highly redundant since, for example, the same sound-events comply with the characters for c-sharp, d-flat, e-triple-flat, b-double-sharp, and so on (181).

Rather, what Goodman must mean in distinguishing between the performance *taken as* an instance of a work, on the one hand, and the performance *taken as* a sound-event, on the other, is that the *compliance-classes* of the supplementary instructions are sound-event classes *as such*. But here he is just mistaken. The performance(SE) is the performance taken as an *acoustic* event—that is, as a sequence of frequencies, intensities, attack envelopes, and so forth.[9] The supplementary instructions, on the other hand, specify values of *perceptual* parameters—pitch, loudness, duration, articulation, *perceived* speed, etc. The compliance-classes of the supplementary instructions contain sound-events as their members, to be sure, but those classes themselves are individuated on perceptual grounds; that is to say, the membership of a given (token) sound-event in a particular compliance-class is determined by the sound-event's *perceptual* properties, not its acoustic ones. In short, Goodman confuses sound-event classes *as such* with perceptual-event classes, and wrongly identifies the former as compliance-classes of the supplementary instructions. This error comes back to haunt him, as we shall soon see.

If not as a sound-event, how *is* the performance to be taken *qua* compliant of the supplementary instructions? The obvious answer, it seems to me, is that the designated values are just our old friends the performance *nuances*, "taken to infinity" as it were. The compliant of the supplementary instructions is the *performance taken as a sequence of nuances*—the performance(N), as I shall call it. The performance(N) is just the performance considered as instantiating a particular determinate sequence of N-pitches, N-durations, N-tempi, N-articulations, and so forth. In what follows I shall replace Goodman's references to the performance(SE) with references to the performance(N). Given the replacement, his claim that the supplementary instructions are semantically dense and undifferentiated is expressible thus: each scheme of supplementary instructions provides for infinitely many nuance (e.g., N-pitch) characters with compliance-classes so ordered that between each two is a third less discriminable from each of them than they are from each other. Understood in this way, the denotation of musical nuances by their respective supplementary instructions issues in the first of Goodman's three ineffabilities: it is not theoretically possible to determine, *a fortiori* to say, which supplementary character any given sound-event-qua-nuance complies with. We may have at hand the requisite repertoire of characters (instructions), and there may be a fact of the matter as to which character a given sound-event-qua-nuance complies with, but in principle there will be no saying which.

Now let's have a look at the pair of ineffabilities spawned by the performance considered as a symbol.

6.1.2 The Performance as Symbol

Unlike Scores and scores, performances typically do not denote. Instead, they exemplify: they function as samples. Goodman distinguishes two species of exemplification—literal and metaphorical—each serving up its characteristic ineffability. Let us consider them in turn.

The exemplifying symbol both instantiates and refers to what it exemplifies: a symbol S exemplifies a property P if and only if 'P' applies to S (i.e., S instantiates P) and S refers to P (53).[10] In particular, a musical performance exemplifies the properties named by the markings that apply to or denote it; specifically, the performance(W) exemplifies the properties named by the notational markings, the performance(N) the properties named by the supplementary ones. Thus the A-naturals in a musical performance exemplify the property of being an A-natural insofar as the A-natural marking (character) applies to them and they refer to the corresponding property; the eighth-notes exemplify the property of being an eighth-note, the loud passages the property of being loud, the slightly high A-naturals the property of being a slightly high A-natural (or, if you prefer, the A-natural(12)'s the property of being an A-natural(12)), and so on.

The idea that the events of a performance instantiate properties of the kind just cited is unproblematic. But how do those events *refer* to those properties? Goodman explains that such reference "is a matter of singling out certain properties for attention, of selecting associations with certain other objects" (88); a symbol need not—indeed, typically does not—exemplify *all* of its properties. A tailor's color swatch, for instance, "is a sample of color, weave, texture, and pattern but not of size, shape, or absolute weight or value" (53); nor *a fortiori* does it exemplify the property of having been finished on a Tuesday. The swatch exemplifies only those properties it refers to—that is, singles out for attention—and it does not refer to the property of having been finished on a certain day of the week. Precisely which of its properties the color swatch refers to is apparently decided by appeal to relevant conventions: we adhere to a convention of using tailors' swatches as samples of color and weave but not of size or shape. By the same token, Goodman seems to think, we adhere to a convention of using pitch-time events as samples of pitch and rhythm but not of, say, the property of being played in New York City or composed at a Mason and Hamlin piano.

I shall register some criticisms of Goodman's exemplification relation in the next section; for the moment our goal is simply to get clear what musical exemplification is and how it spawns the second of the three ineffabilities that arise on his analysis. In that regard it should not surprise us to find that, in its exemplification of the properties named by the Scored notational markings, the performance(W) is syntactically and semantically disjoint, differentiated, and nondense; whereas in its exemplification of the properties named by the supplementary instructions, the performance(N) is semantically dense and undifferentiated: for example, between any two N-pitches (N-pitch "properties") there is theoretically a third less discriminable from each of them than they are from each other. Hence it is in principle impossible to determine, for any given sound-event in a performance, which nuance property it exemplifies:

> [D]espite the definition of works by Scores, exemplification... of anything beyond the Score is reference in a syntactically and semantically dense system, and a matter of infinitely fine adjustment (237-238).

We have so far characterized the literal exemplification of musical properties by musical performances. More mysterious still is the *metaphorical* exemplification or *expression* of certain "affective" or "stylistic" properties not typically prescribed either by the Score or by the supplementary instructions—properties like sadness, fragility, and heroism.

The subject of metaphor has inspired many volumes in recent years, and a thorough consideration of it would take us far afield of our project here; however, we shall need at least a superficial familiarity with Goodman's conception of the device.

On Goodman's view, a symbol S expresses a property P if and only if P metaphorically applies to S and S refers to P. What is it for a predicate 'P' to apply metaphorically to something? We are told that metaphor consists in "applying an old label in a new way" (69)—not simply to new cases, but in a new way. Whereas we may apply an old label to new or hitherto undecided cases by "routine projection" (or, of course, a newly coined label to its newly minted extension), metaphor depends on flouting "an express or tacit denial of that label to that object. Where there is metaphor, there is conflict" (69). Metaphor involves the "migration" of a label—or, more properly, a set of related labels—from one domain of reference to another.

Musical expression is the business of the performance(N). The expressed properties ride piggyback, as it were, on the nuances denoted by the supplementary instructions:

> A musical performance also normally exemplifies and expresses much beside the work or Score. A property may be said elliptically to be exemplified by the work if exemplified by all performances of the work. But this will seldom happen, since exemplified properties not prescribed by the Score are nonconstitutive and may vary freely from performance to performance without affecting the status of any performance as a genuine (even if reprehensible) instance of the work. That we may have a limp performance of a heroic work is all too evident. What, though, can be meant here by saying the work is heroic? If we answer that to say the work is heroic is to say elliptically that all its *proper* performances are, "proper" cannot mean merely "compliant with the Score." The propriety in question is rather compliance with supplementary instructions, verbal or otherwise, either printed along with the Score or tacitly given by tradition, word-of-mouth, etc. We have seen [that] these instructions [cannot] be taken as integral parts of the Score, for they belong to a syntactically unlimited and semantically dense system, not to a notational language. And since performances taken as sound-events rather than as instances of works are not fully dif-

ferentiated, exemplification of whatever is not prescribed by the Score is, like pictorial exemplification, a matter of inverted gauging or measuring[11] (237–238).

Though Goodman supplies no examples, one imagines that a performance would express (i.e., metaphorically exemplify) the property of being sad in virtue of complying with supplementary markings like *'pianissimo'* (very soft), *'largo'* (quite slow), 'Play that A-natural slightly lower', and so on, while a heroic performance might comply with markings like *'fortissimo'* (very loud), *'moderato'* (moderate in speed), and 'Play that A-natural slightly higher'.

Goodman's analysis of musical expression seems to me highly problematic, and I shall say why momentarily. For now the important point is that, as he sees it, the properties expressed by a performance belong to dense and undifferentiated reference-classes, therein giving rise to a third species of ineffability. Just as there are in theory infinitely many N-pitches (N-pitch properties) so ordered that between any two is a third less discriminable from each of them than they are from each other, there are in theory infinitely many degrees of, say, sadness (e.g., moderate sadness, great sadness, between moderate and great sadness, between moderate and between-moderate-and-great-sadness, etc.) so ordered that between any two is a third less discriminable from each of them than they are from each other. As a result, the musical expression of such properties is ineffable: it is not even theoretically possible to determine, nor hence to say, what degree of sadness a given performance(N) expresses.

These then are the three loci of musical ineffability that emerge on Goodman's analysis as I understand it:

(I-a) The denotation of the performance(N) by supplementary instructions

(I-b) The literal exemplification of "nuance" properties by the performance(N)

(I-c) The metaphorical exemplification (expression) of "stylistic" or "affective" properties by the performance(N).

Via one avenue or another, each of the three ineffabilities is born of the density and undifferentiatedness of the supplementary instructions: it is in theory impossible to determine which nuances are denoted, which properties are exemplified, which properties are expressed.

6.2 Part Two: The Intersection

We are now positioned to undertake our second task—viz., that of indicating where Goodman's theory and our cognitivist one come together. It must be obvious that, with minor disparities, Goodman's performance(W) is the performance as represented in the mental score, while the performance(N) is the performance as represented in the N-level. Moreover, just as we located the nuance ineffability in certain features of performances as opposed to works, Goodman takes a similar line: as we have heard, the performance(N) is the denotatum or compliant of the supplementary instructions, and these latter

> cannot be accounted integral parts of the defining Score, but are rather auxiliary directions whose observance or nonobservance affects the quality of a performance but not the identity of the work (185)....[For example,] exemplified properties not prescribed by the Score are nonconstitutive and may vary freely from performance to performance without affecting the status of any performance as a genuine (even if reprehensible) instance of the work (237).

At the very least, then, Goodman's account and our cognitivist one trace the ineffability of music to the same neighborhood.[12] However, Goodman's theory yields three sources of ineffability which differ from one another in non-trivial ways. Where precisely is the parallel to be drawn?

It seems to me that (I-b) and (I-c) are inadequate, not just as sources of ineffability, but indeed as symbolic relations altogether. Does an eighth note single out for attention the property of being an eighth note, or a *legato* passage the property of being *legato*? Does the second movement of the Tchaikovsky *Serenade in C* function as a *sample* of compound meter, or the final bars of his sixth symphony as a *sample* of loudness? Such a view has no obvious basis in either common sense or musical intuition, and absent a compelling defense by Goodman we have no reason whatever to embrace it. The events of a performance *are* eighth notes, or *legato*, or very loud, or slightly high; but they do not typically *refer* to those properties, even in Goodman's "attentional" sense of the term. Granted, our attention may in fact be attracted to certain nuances rather than others at any given moment in a performance (e.g., one may notice loudness more than tempo at some places, *vice versa* at others), depending on how the performer chooses to handle things; indeed, I have taken pains to emphasize precisely that we *do* attend to these fine-grained "expressive" features. But it hardly follows that they are singled out for our attention. (Though Goodman would surely wince at this way of putting it, *singling out for attention* must be an *in*tentional notion.) Rather, the production of musical nuances is a means to an end; one might say that the nuances are used, not mentioned, in the service of communicating an interpretation of a work. Composer and performer alike strive not to make us attend to the nuances *per se*, but rather by controlling the nuances to make us attend to the *structural* features of the music—that is, to the *work*. By the skillful manipulation of these fine-grained details, the performer "guides our ears" to the phrase boundaries, "points out" that one pitch is a prolongation of another, "alerts us" that a certain eighth note is preparatory to the downbeat. Nor is this to suggest that the structural properties themselves are exemplified; whatever the performance may be doing, it is not typically functioning as a sample of *anything*. Maybe a "minimalist" work like Terry Riley's *In C* (43 minutes of arpeggiated C major chord) exemplifies C major, or Cage's *4'33"* exemplifies silence (among other things); but surely such works are the exception rather than the rule.

Prima facie the idea that a performance expresses properties like sadness and heroism has more to recommend it. To begin with, composers sometimes say they intend their music, and performers their performances, to express certain "affective" or "stylistic" properties; and as we saw in chapter 3, listeners (especially some philosophers!) often view music as serving such communicative ends. Furthermore, musicians sometimes talk as if the supposed heroism or sadness of a performance depends upon its nuances: one wants to play the music slower at a certain place *in order that it be* sad, or very loud in a certain passage *in order that it be* heroic, and so on. So although I do not find it plausible in general to say that a performance singles out its loudness for attention, there is at least some independent motivation for claiming that the performance *is* loud in order to single out its (metaphorical) heroism.

Unfortunately, that is about all Goodman's notion of musical expression has to recommend it. Even supposing that we do adhere to conventional associations of loud dynamic levels, marcato articulations, and moderate speeds with heroism, or soft dynamic levels, legato articulations, and slow speeds with sadness, the vast majority of tonal music (not to mention the atonal varieties) sustains no such associations at all. On Goodman's view it would seem to follow that the vast majority of music is not expressive—an unpalatable result at best. I do not deny that such a line could be defended, but it is far from obvious how the argument would go. To boot, Goodman offers no reason why the expressed properties depend upon nonnotated (nuance) features of a performance as opposed to notated (structural) ones--a lapse that is especially puzzling inasmuch as the best entrenched of our "conventional associations" make major keys happy and minor keys sad.

Pending further elaboration by Goodman, then, we set aside (I-b) and (I-c) as musical symbolic relations and, therewith, as sources of ineffability.[13] That leaves (I-a), the denotation of musical nuances by supplementary instructions. As you may have guessed, here is where Goodman's analysis and our cognitivist theory of nuance ineffability converge. Granted, Goodman's ineffability is supposed to be a "theoretical" or "logical" ineffability resulting from the semantic density and undifferentiatedness of the supplementary instructions, whereas our ineffability is at least *prima facie* a merely psychological one. Nevertheless, as I shall show in §6.4, this apparent gulf between the two stories shrinks to nothing—or anyway nothing very important—in the end.

First, though, I want to flag a potential trouble spot in Goodman's analysis.

6.3 Part Three: The Worry

Goodman's treatment of the Score as a notational system seems to me straightforward and plausible; at any rate, I shall not contest it here. His treatment of the supplementary instructions, on the other hand— in particular, his claim that they are semantically dense—should give us pause. After all, pitches and dynamics and durations and the rest are *perceptual* properties, and perceptual systems, whatever their precise nature, are decidedly limited: even the most sensitive ear can discriminate only finitely many values along the various dimensions of auditory perception. How then can these latter sustain dense orderings?

The answer may at first seem obvious. As Goodman explains, "[s]emantic density requires only that a dense set of [compliance]-classes be *provided for*, not that the field of [compliance] be *actually* dense" (227). However, one may question even the possibility of *providing for* a dense set of classes along perceptual dimensions. Consider pitch, for example. Different pitches are, by their nature, *discriminably* different: sound-events are different (/identical) in pitch only if they sound different (/identical) to normal observers under normal conditions (whatever 'normal' comes to), just as objects are different in color only if they look different. Thus the theoretical possibility of a dense ordering of pitches presupposes the theoretical possibility of a listener endowed with an infinitely sensitive discriminatory capacity. The question then arises: *is* such a listener theoretically possible?

One might, just for instance, reason in the following way. Consider that we never hear instances of (say) A-natural *simpliciter*, any more than we see instances of red *simpliciter*. In a perfectly clear sense, we hear only *particular determinate* A-naturals, see only *particular determinate* reds (viz. shades of red). To put the point another way: any pitch determinable (e.g., A-natural, B-flat, C-sharp) is a general category with which we are perceptually "acquainted" only via our perceptual acquaintance with (tokens of) its determinate values. Perhaps we can say: hearing an A-natural as such consists in hearing some particular determinate pitch *as* an A-natural, just as seeing a red object as such consists in seeing its particular determinate shade *as* red. Given the inevitable disparities in our discrimination profiles, you may hear a greater number of determinate pitches than I; but each of us hears, in the sense at issue, whatever are the finest values he can discriminate (at the time). I cannot prove the latter claim, but it seems to express a truth about perception that transcends any special features of *homo sapiens:* in general, the values that can be perceived along a given dimension are the finest values that can be discriminated.

Now a dense ordering of pitches would map them one-to-one into (a closed interval of) the rational numbers. (Suppose that order and relative distances are preserved.) It seems to follow that in such a case there would be no finest discriminable values: just as there is no "finest" difference between rational numbers, there would be no finest difference between densely ordered pitches. And this is presumably to say: there would be no *determinate* pitches. But if that is right, then given the contention of the preceding paragraph, no one—not even an infinitely sensitive discriminator—could hear pitches that were densely ordered. And pitches that can't be heard aren't pitches at all. Thus there is no even theoretical possibility of a dense ordering of pitches (durations, dynamics, articulations, etc.) to fund Goodman's analysis of musical ineffability. Or so one might contend.

Of course the foregoing is at best the sketch of an argument, and even if it gets things roughly right, a great deal more would need to be said. Much will depend upon the way in which determinate values are individuated along perceptual dimensions, and given such perplexities as the nontransitivity of the indistinguishability relation, the situation gets very knotty very fast. But that is really just my present point— viz., that an appeal to densely ordered perceptual values would require extended and meticulous defense. Goodman offers neither. The reason for this lapse, I surmise, is precisely his failure to reckon with the *perceptual* nature of the values involved. I shall return to this point momentarily.

Perhaps Goodman would object that our pretheoretic conception of pitch discrimination is too narrow. Granted, he might say, the degree to which the pitches of two tones can resemble one another *when the tones are considered pairwise* is highly limited: even the best of listeners, under the best of circumstances, can discriminate only several hundred steps of pitch difference within a semitone. Nevertheless, there may be the following "indirect" route whereby pitches could be densely ordered. Consider that for any two distinct frequencies F1 and F2, there will always be some third frequency (indeed, infinitely many frequencies) F3 such that tokens of F1 are discriminable from tokens of F3 but tokens of F2 are not. (Just what F3 is will vary both intra- and intersubjectively, but some such frequency will always be specifiable in theory.) To that extent, tokens of any two different frequencies are discriminably different; that is to say, they differ in pitch. The compelling intuition that pairwise indiscriminable frequencies are identical in pitch is simply mistaken; other, less direct though still perceptual, evidence can be mobilized to map pitches one-to-one into acoustic frequencies in a dense ordering.[14]

Ingenious though it may be, such a proposal does little to alleviate the present worry. For whether or not the described individuation specifies a dense ordering of *perceptual* classes at all (cf., e.g., Dummett 1975), it certainly does not specify a dense ordering of the kinds of pitch-classes required by Goodman's analysis. The requisite classes, recall, are those complying with the supplementary instructions for performance. And the point is, the teacher who asks his student for an A-natural *slightly higher* than one just played will not be satisfied—his directive will not have been met—by a second A-natural that is pairwise indiscriminable from the first. Slightly higher A-naturals are *pairwise discriminably higher,* and a pitch that lies between a "good" A-natural and a slightly high A-natural, or between an A-natural(11) and an A-natural(12), must be *directly* discriminably higher than the one and lower than the other.

One may ask why we cannot theorize about infinitely fine pitch discriminations in the way that linguists sometimes theorize about the grammatical generation of infinitely many sentences. Can't we invoke an analogous idealization in the musical case?[15] I don't think so. The principles of grammatical sentence construction can be specified in a purely formal way independently of any appeal to an understander, theoretical or otherwise. By contrast, pitch is an essentially psychological parameter: different pitches have got to be *discriminably* different—that is, different to some (at least theoretically possible) listener. That makes theorizing about infinitely sensitive pitch discrimination a different kettle of fish from theorizing about the generation of infinitely many sentences.

It is worth emphasizing that appeal to the theoretical possibility of an *indefinitely* sensitive discriminator—that is, a discriminator such that, for any two distinct pitches, it could in theory be made sufficiently sensitive to detect the difference—is of no help to Goodman here. As he himself warns:

> So long as the differentiation between characters is finite, no matter how minute, the determination of membership of mark in

character will depend upon the acuteness of our perceptions and the sensitivity of the instruments we can devise (135).

In other words, in such a case the characters will not be densely ordered, nor will a dense ordering even be "provided for." Presumably the same holds for their compliance-classes.

At the root of Goodman's apparent troubles here, I suspect, is a mistake to which I have already alluded. In identifying the compliant of the supplementary markings with the performance-taken-as-a-sound-event, he illicitly transports features of the acoustic realm into the perceptual; in particular, he mistakes a dense ordering of frequency-classes for a dense ordering of pitch-classes. And of course there is no problem about a dense ordering of frequencies: between any two is a third less discriminable from each of them than they are from each other. The problem is that Goodman's analysis requires not a dense ordering of frequencies as such, but rather a dense ordering of the pitch-classes of which (tokens of) those frequencies are members.

Inviting this slip is a more general misconception that reverberates throughout *Languages of Art*. Goodman aims to *analyze* the various symbolic relations effective in the arts, and he insists upon a sharp segregation of his "theoretical" concerns from merely "applied" or "practical"—for example, psychological—ones. The following remarks are characteristic:

> The...stated requirements for a notational system are all negative and general, satisfiable by systems with null or even no [syntactic] characters....A good many other features that might be thought essential are not covered...No requirement of a manageably small or even finite set of atomic characters, no requirement of clarity, of legibility, of durability, of maneuverability, of ease of writing or reading, of graphic suggestiveness, of mnemonic efficacy, or of ready duplicability or performability has been imposed. These may be highly desirable properties, and to some degree even necessary for any practicable notation; and the study of such engineering matters could be fascinating and profitable. But none of this has anything to do with the basic theoretical function of notation systems (154).

I am by no means claiming that the details of the pictorial systems are before us for easy discovery; and I have offered no aid in deciding whether a given picture exemplifies a given property...but only an analysis of the symbolic relation...of pictorial exemplification where [it] may obtain (236).

In this connection, Goodman has been reprimanded for missing the true senses of (at least some of) the terms at issue. Consider for instance John Haugeland's unhappiness with his treatment of digital symbols:

In making his determinations "theoretically possible," without mentioning the determination procedures, let alone the production procedures or the working conditions, Goodman betrays a mathematician's distaste for the nitty-gritty of *practical* devices. But *digital*, like *accurate, economical*, or *heavy-duty*, is a mundane engineering notion, root and branch. It only makes sense as a practical means to cope with the vagaries and vicissitudes, the noise and drift, of earthly existence (1982, 217).

Haugeland's point is well taken, it seems to me, and at present I am airing a related concern. That is, that Goodman's theoretical purism blinds him to the fact that artworks and artistic activity in general are shot through with the "noise and drift" of our limited human psychology. When the compliance-classes at issue are *essentially* perceptual in nature, the determination procedures cannot be ignored.

6.4 Part Four: The Realization

Even if Goodman's analysis *is* finally defeated by the limits of sense-perception, the strong kinship between his ineffability source (I-a) and our notion of nuance ineffability suggests that the philosophical marrow of his account, if not its particulars, can be preserved. Goodman has told us that (syntactic and/or semantic) undifferentiatedness "may carry some suggestion of the ineffability so often claimed for, or charged against, the aesthetic," and that "ineffability upon analysis turns into density rather than mystery" (253). In this final section, I shall show that our cognitivist story provides a psychologistic reconstruction of both of these claims.

To come straight to the point: while there may be no principled speechlessness of the sort Goodman yearns for, it seems entirely reasonable to say that, *as far as the listener's real-time musical experience is concerned*, the nuances (nuance-classes) of the performance(N) are—or anyway *might as well* be—densely ordered. Consider again the mental recovery of pitch and interval nuances in the N-level. Because the music processor institutes schema-driven classification only at the more abstract level of the mental score, the fine shades of difference between the various pitches and intervals recovered in the N-level could *for all the processor cares* be "infinitesimally" small. In more Goodmanian terms: because the music processor institutes schema-driven finite determinations only in its representation of the acoustic signal as a performance(W), in its shallower representation of the signal as a performance(N) "no magnitude of difference in any respect is set as the threshold of significance" *for the listener*. Goodman says of dense systems: "Differences of all kinds and degrees, *measurable or not*, are on equal footing" (193; my emphasis). We say of the N-level: *Audible* differences of all kinds and degrees are on equal footing. Admittedly, frequency and frequency ratio differences smaller than the relevant JNDs are *ipso facto* inaudible, and hence not "on equal footing" with the differences one can hear. But a JND does not, from the listener's preeminent point of view, constitute a "threshold of significance." Rather, a JND reflects a brute threshold of sensitivity in the peripheral transducer. Relative to this mere hardware threshold, the semitone— the basic unit of our tonal pitch system—is the significant threshold. (Remember that the auditory transducer is not a component of the musical grammar—that is, not strictly speaking a component of the system that *understands* the music.) To put the point another way: as far as the music processor is concerned, there is no significant threshold, no significant minimum difference in pitch or interval width, represented in the N-level.

In our cognitivist framework, then, the semantic density of the supplementary instructions "turns into" the absence of a threshold of significant difference in the N-level; at this shallow level of representation, all audible differences are "on equal footing." The semantic undifferentiatedness of the supplementary instructions turns into the psychological impossibility of type-identifying their designated (compliant) nuances, as such, by ear. Goodman's view and our cognitivist story thus come together in the end: musical ineffability (or at least one species of it) consists in the impossibility of identifying, hence of saying, which nuance value we are hearing at any given moment in a musical performance.

At first blush, our reconstructed density and undifferentiatedness may seem merely psychological in nature, not logical or theoretical as Goodman would have it; surely it is theoretically possible that we should be so designed as to have, or be able to acquire, schemas as fine-grained as the nuances we can hear. Upon further reflection, however, one may be inclined to reason in the following (thoroughly Goodmanian) way. Insofar as our musical schemas are responsible for the way tonal music sounds to us, the activation of N-interval schemas in music perception would probably alter the character of that perception. Indeed, as I observed in chapter 5 (§5.1), it is not clear that in such a circumstance we would perceive tonal music, as such, at all. Among other things, it seems likely that every pitch heard in a performance would be *recognized*, and the structures that constitute the work would recede into the background wash. In particular, one might suppose that we would no longer hear any N-pitches or N-intervals as such: nuances, after all, are within-category differences, and within-category differences are differences that do not get recognized or type-identified except as differences within certain categories (here, C-pitch and C-interval categories). Consequently, given the perceptual constitution of properties like pitch and interval width, the very act of type-identifying ("finitely determining") a heard pitch or interval would abort its compliance with any supplementary instruction. Supplementary instructions designate pitch and interval *nuances*, within-category differences: the difference between a "good" A-natural and a slightly high A-natural, or between an A-natural(11) and an A-natural(12), is a fine shade of difference within the C-pitch category A-natural. Thus *to that extent*, one might contend, there is no even theoretical possibility of determining, by ear, the supplementary (nuance) compliance-class of any given sound-event in a performance of a tonal work. Nuances, *qua* nuances, cannot be type-identified.

Understood in this way, our naturalized density and undifferentiatedness may do more justice to Goodman's purely theoretical notions than one would initially have supposed.[16] Of course, it remains to be seen just what implications this revisionary picture will have for the rest of Goodman's theory of symbolism in the arts; but that investigation must await another time and place. For now, I hope to have shown that our cognitivist story preserves the central insight of Goodman's analysis of musical ineffability. I said at the outset that his theory would be "rediscovered and vindicated" by the present account; but of course the vindication, if such it be, goes both ways.

Chapter 7

Qualms About Quining Qualia

As Anscombe would put it, we simply can say *what it is we are experiencing . . .*

Daniel Dennett 1978, 170

Like their progenitors in the philosophy of art, the arguments of chapters 1 through 6 have focused primarily on the relationship between effability and (conscious musical) knowledge. In particular, they have treated only indirectly the relationship between effability and *consciousness per se.* But of course a time-honored view in the cognitive sciences has consciousness itself bound up in some intimate, perhaps essential way with the ability to make verbal reports. As Patricia Churchland observes, "[t]he idea . . . of [a] special relation between consciousness and linguistic competence . . . is widespread, and may perhaps be granted the status of conventional wisdom" (1983, 81).

The nature of conscious experience is perhaps the biggest—certainly the scariest—conundrum facing theorists of mind today. In a nutshell, it is hard to see how any broadly materialistic theory could accommodate (/capture/include/do justice to) the so-called subjective or phenomenological characteristics of our conscious states. Or so many philosophers contend (cf. Nagel 1974, Jackson 1982, 1986, e.g.). Thomas Nagel sums up the situation with characteristic punch: "Without consciousness the mind-body problem would be much less interesting. With consciousness it seems hopeless" (1974, 166). As a result, verbalizability is often said to be *criterial* of conscious access, while questions about the nature of consciousness itself are left judiciously to one side. In recent years, however, at least one intrepid philosopher has dared to look the "quicksilver of phenomenology" square in the eye, taking the conventional wisdom to extremes: consciousness, Daniel Dennett maintains, just *consists in* a sequence of "propositional episodes" or "judgments" or "intentions-to- say-that-p." The raw feels and spinning images of pretheoretic intuition are but convenient fictions: there is no phenomenology in the usual sense of the term.[1]

Not surprisingly, Dennett's mental minimalism has met with its share of resistance, not to say hostility: "Surely he's left something out! Surely he's failed to capture what it's like to experience the colors and sounds and tastes and textures of the world around us!" But of course this familiar rallying cry is no more than an airing of intuitions and so cuts little ice against the likes of Dennett, whose intuitions tilt in a radically different direction. Moreover, it proves nightmarishly difficult to say just what it *is* that gets "left out" by theories like Dennett's. For instance, little progress has been made toward an understanding of so-called phenomenal space (the mental arena or "inner theatre" wherein experience is often supposed to occur), or of how its occupants could have the properties standardly ascribed to them—viz. phenomenal extendedness and motion, and phenomenal colors, pitches, and tastes (a.k.a. *qualia*), to name just a few. *A fortiori* the outlook is grim for an understanding of how a mind so endowed could be accounted for within the materialistic ken of the natural sciences.[2] We shall need to keep this feature of the dialectic in mind as we go along: given the staggering theoretical obstacles faced by patrons of the inner theatre, Dennett will have a leg up if he can persuade us simply that consciousness *could be* as he describes it.

That said, my (largely negative) ambition here is to show that the nuance ineffability of musical performances suggests an independent line of attack against Dennett—a line that does not, at least not on the face of it, require the endorsement of a phenomenology and its problematic accessories. Dennett's theory leaves something out all right; but what it leaves out is the conscious *representational* (as opposed to: *phenomenological)* content of the N-level. Specifically, I shall try to show that our apparent lack of N-interval schemas blocks the path of any account that would cast the conscious content of the N-level in "propositional" form. This is not to say that I oppose Dennett's eliminativist line altogether; on the contrary, his approach seems to me highly promising. Hence in the end I shall urge that we seek a path that preserves the eliminative thrust of his view while somehow—and I do not profess to know how—making room for "nonpropositional" representations in conscious awareness.

I warned in chapter 1 that the proportion of quoted material in this book would be high in places. That caveat is especially applicable to the present chapter, for at least two reasons. First, Dennett's theory flies in the face of cherished pretheoretic intuitions about the nature of conscious experience; hence the reader hitherto unacquainted with it is likely to doubt the fidelity of any paraphrase and will want to see the textual evidence for himself. Second, like any large-scale creative endeavor, Dennett's view has undergone a variety of transformations over the years. My aim here is to isolate one important and recurrent theme in his writing—roughly, the idea that consciousness is propositional in form—and to show how it is cast into doubt by our story of the nuance ineffability. Part of my task, then, will be to trace this theme through a number of Dennett's papers; and the results of that exegetical detective work too will want textual defense.

7.1 Dennett's Propositionalist Program

First of all, just what are these so-called propositional episodes? We find the following:

> If you have ever had a sudden *presentiment* that someone was looking over your shoulder, or a *premonition* that something dire was about to happen, you are acquainted with my topic. These are examples *par excellence* of the sort of propositional episode I have in mind: they are *propositional*—that is, they are thinkings that p; there is normally some inclination to express them (though the inclination is easily suppressed or canceled); and when they occur in us we haven't the faintest idea what their etiology is (. . . my point is that 'to introspection' they arrive from we know not where) . . . . Needing a convenient term for these episodes, I call them judgments (1979, 94-95).[3]

Typically these episodes are momentary, wordless thinkings or convictions (sometimes misleadingly called conscious or episodic beliefs) that are often supposed to be the executive bridges leading

to our public, worded introspective reports from our perusal . . .
of the phenomenological manifold our reports are about. My view,
put bluntly, is that there is no phenomenological manifold in any
such relation to our reports. There are public reports we issue, and
then there are the episodes of our propositional awareness, our
judgments, and then there is—so far as introspection is concerned—
darkness (1979, 95).

[T]here are no colours, images, sounds, gestalts, mental acts, feeling tones or other Proustian *objets trouvés* to delight the inner eye;
only featureless—even wordless—conditional-intentions-to-say-
that-p for us to be intimately acquainted with (1979, 97).

[I]f we say what we mean to say, if we have committed no errors
or infelicities of expression, then our actual utterances cannot fail
to be expressions of the content of our semantic intentions, cannot
fail to do justice to the access we have to our own inner lives (1978,
171).

A bracingly Spartan portrait of conscious experience! Between subter-
ranean brain processes and explicit verbal reports are, solely, tokenings
of some sort of proto-linguistic objects—"judgments," "intentions-
to-say-that-p." These exhaust our conscious awareness.

That the judgments in question are propositional appears to be a claim
about their *format* as well as their content. Or at any rate, if their format
is not propositional in the sense of *sentential* (i.e., in the sense of having
subject and predicate terms), at least it is "nonpresentational,"
"nonanalogue," "nonimagistic," "nonisomorphic" to whatever it is that
the judgments are about. (For example, *modulo* the right sorts of sys-
temic stipulations, numerals for natural numbers could be paired with
determinate hues in such a way that '1' carries the propositional content
that a certain object O is a certain determinate shade of blue, '2' the content
that O is a certain (different) determinate shade of blue, and so on; such a
code would be nonsentential but also "nonpresentational" in format.
I take Dennett to mean 'propositional' in a liberal sense that would
allow numerical codes *inter alia.*) We might put the point this way:
whatever exactly the format of these judgments may be, no systematic
relationship (*a fortiori* no isomorphism) obtains between it and the
"formats" of the things the judgments are about. The judgments about

one's (putative) purple cow images are no more purple or cow-shaped than are the judgments about one's tonic triad experiences in-tune or out.[4] Reflecting upon the experience of phosphenes (those colored shapes one "sees" upon pressing one's fingers to one's eyeballs), Dennett writes:

> [T]hough I can grant the claim that 'seeing' phosphenes is importantly similar 'introspectively' to seeing a checkerboard undulating . . . I do not thereby grant the appropriateness of the question 'So where are the square coloured things'? What I grant is that the same judgments (roughly) occur in both experiences, and they (the judgments) are not square or coloured . . . . Now whatever it is that accomplishes phosphene production . . . might turn out to be an internal image-utilizing information-processing system (the images would be actual topological regions of excitation or whatever, relatively close to the retina). If so, then these fields of excitation would have properties isomorphic to colour and shape, which would constrain and determine our judgments about the 'colour and shape' of phosphenes and memory image items, but if there are such images, they are not anything to which we have privileged access, are not 'objects of consciousness' and of course do not occupy 'phenomenal space' but real space (1979, 107-108).

Indeed, *only* a claim about the format of our conscious representations could raze the phenomenological landscape in the way Dennett envisions, for it is (some among) the putative *vehicles* of conscious content, as opposed to that content itself, that are supposed to have phenomenal properties. And it is generally agreed that whereas conscious *images* (*presentations/analogues/isomorphs*) would have properties like phenomenal color and shape (whatever those are), or phenomenal pitch and loudness (whatever those are), conscious *"propositions"* would be phenomenologically naked. (Consider that whereas the propositional content *that O is blue #2* can be borne by a picture of O, by the sentence 'O is blue #2', and by the numeral '2', among others, typically only the first of these representations would itself *be* blue.) Hence the motivation for supplanting talk of mental images and the rest with talk of mental propositions in a theory of consciousness. Presumably the virtue of restricting the *content* of awareness to propositional (or otherwise "judgmental") content is that such content is guaranteed *a priori* to admit of carriage in a propositional format.

We often fancy our introspective access accomplished by an inner eye which surveys the neural goings-on via their projections (raw feels, mental images) onto some mental movie screen, much as Plato's cave-dwellers survey reality in its shadows on the wall. But this home-grown picture, Dennett insists, is just so much make-believe. The *brain* may do *something like* rotate *something like* an image; just for example, the well known Shepard and Metzler (1971) image rotation data strongly suggest the operation of imagic or image-like processes. But Dennett's point is that such neural "rotations," if they transpire at all, are not *experienced*: we have no introspective access to them. When it seems to me for all the world that I am consciously experiencing the rotation of a mental image, in fact I am only "visited by a series of judgments which [I] find it irresistible to interpret as issuing somehow from something like the apprehension of an image" (1979, 105):

> Aren't we directly aware of an image rotating in phenomenal space? No . . . . For isn't it the case that if you attend to your experience more closely when you say you rotate the image you find it moves in discrete jumps—it flicks through a series of orientations . . . . But now look again. Isn't it really just that these discrete steps are discrete propositional episodes: now it looks like *this*, but if I imagine it turned *that* much, it would look like that. . . . One reply that suggests itself is that these judgments have to be about something, and in particular, when I express them, as I did, in such words as 'now it looks like *this*, now it looks like *that*,' what can I be ostending or referring to with these demonstratives, if not to some image? . . . .[W]hat is the force of the 'this' and 'that'? In the case of the duck-rabbit, the answer is simple: now it looks like a duck, now like a rabbit. When it comes to the Necker cube the words are harder to come by: now it looks as if its near face is up and right, now it looks as if its near face is down and left. When it comes to the judgments about the rotating images the words are still harder to get in order, but it is to the execution of that task that our 'this' and 'that' are promissory notes. Or almost. For if someone really wanted to know what I *meant* by the 'this' and 'that' in my protocol, I might find it *more convenient* to convey what I meant by

drawing a picture for him, but if I did this, I would not be drawing a replica of what I was aware of, nor could my drawing, in virtue of being a drawing, stand in a relation of any 'higher fidelity' to the mental state I would be trying to communicate (1979, 104-106).

So: the demonstratives in my protocols are not really *demonstratives* at all—or at least they are not demonstratives trained on any phenomenological objects. But then what do I *mean* by my 'this' and 'that'? The idea seems to be that, in theory, the protocols containing these verbal pointers can always be followed up by protocols that eliminate them, explicitly spelling out what I meant by them: by 'like this' I meant 'like a duck', by 'like that' I meant 'like a rabbit'. On such a picture, 'this' and 'that' must be flags for clusters of judgments (propositional episodes) available for enunciation, as if waiting in a queue. Or maybe in some cases they flag judgments for whose verbal expression I have not yet learned the requisite terms (e.g. 'Now it sounds like a major sixth', or 'Now I'm having a déjà-vu experience'). Either way, the contents of my conscious awareness are in theory exhaustively reportable: with sufficient time and mastery of vocabulary I could "linguify" them completely. To put the point another way, the contents of the judgments whose tokenings constitute conscious awareness just are the sorts of things that can be *said* by the subject having them. Admittedly, if someone pressed me to specify what I meant by 'this' and 'that' in the image rotation case, I might wisely forego any attempt to enunciate those many complex judgments, favoring instead a more artistic mode of expression. But such a strategy would be a concession to mere convenience: if I really put my mind to it, I could report exhaustively the contents of my conscious awareness.

7.2 Exeunt Qualia

A similarly stark picture emerges in "Quining Qualia"[5] (1988), Dennett's long-awaited requiem for raw feels. If you have ever entertained the possibility of intersubjective spectrum inversion—that is, the possibility that (for example) the way red looks to you is the way green looks to your companion, and *vice versa*, though there is in principle no way to detect the difference between you—you were entertaining the possibility that your respective color *qualia* might be inverted. Qualia are typically characterized by their defenders as *inter alia* intrinsic, ineffable, private, immediately (hence incorrigibly) apprehensible properties of the mental states to which they adhere—and a reef on which any materialist theory of mind is doomed to founder. At the same time, their reputed possession of such mysterious attributes has made qualia the target of numerous attacks. In "Quining Qualia," Dennett spins a series of arguments designed to show that nothing could instantiate the quartet of properties just mentioned; there simply are no qualia.

Much can be said both for and against the vision that emerges in this famous paper, but at present I am interested only in the following. According to Dennett, what underlies and inspires our misguided talk about qualia are in fact just humdrum informational (ultimately neural) properties of our sense-perceptions—"phenomenal information properties" or "pips," he calls them. Preparing an analogy with "the old spy trick" of tearing a Jello box in two as an improvement on identification by password, Dennett observes that "the particular jagged edge of one piece becomes a *practically* unique pattern-recognition device for its mate; it is an apparatus for detecting the shape property M, where M is uniquely instantiated by its mate" (1988, 69). In similar fashion, the pips of a sensory-perceptual state become a practically unique pattern-recognition device for some property M of the relevant causative stimulus. For example, the pips of your perception of an E-natural guitar tone become a practically unique pattern-recognition device for instances of that property (viz., the property of being an E-natural guitar tone). As I understand it, the pips of your state are those elements of its "shape"—be they spiking frequencies, voltage levels, activation patterns, or whatever—that carry recognitional information about the various perceived features of the stimulus. For instance, the pips carry the kind of information about frequency and waveform, that enables you, with a bit of practice, to recognize heard stimuli as E-natural guitar tones.

Now if I read Dennett correctly, our conscious access to the contents of our sensory-perceptual states derives solely from their pips'

> power to provoke in [us] acts of (apparent) re-identification or recognition. This power is of course a Lockean, dispositional property on a par with the power of bitter things to provoke a certain

reaction in people. It is this power alone, however it might be realized in the brain, that gives [us] 'access' to the deliverances of [our] individual property detectors . . . .We do not have to know how we identify or re-identify or gain access to such internal response types in order to be able so to identify them . . . . The properties of the 'thing experienced' are not to be confused with the properties of the event that realizes the experiencing. To put the matter vividly, the physical difference between someone's imagining a purple cow and imagining a green cow might be nothing more than the presence or absence of a particular zero or one in one of the brain's 'registers'. Such a brute physical presence is all that it would take to anchor the sorts of dispositional differences between imagining a purple cow and imagining a green cow that could then flow, causally, from that 'intrinsic' fact (1988, 70-71).

Evidently conscious awareness of the contents of one's sensory-perceptual states consists in the making of certain *judgments* ("acts of apparent re-identification or recognition") about those states—judgments "provoked" by their pips. For example: 'I am now having the same kind of taste experience that I had yesterday', 'I am now rotating an image of a purple cow', 'I am now perceiving an E-natural guitar tone'. Acts of re-identification or recognition are, presumably, acts of type-identification; and acts of type-identification are presumably just the sort of thing that can be rendered in propositional form and, ultimately, expressed in a sentence of the natural language. As before, consciousness appears to be a wholly propositional affair.[6]

Again, Dennett allows that our talk of qualia may be inspired by real features of the underlying brainscape. Perhaps the reputed *privacy* of qualia can be "reformulated" as the "idiosyncrasy of our discrimination profiles" (1988, 69), and the *atomicity* of qualia as the cognitive impenetrability of our dispositions to identify and re-identify our sensory-perceptual states at any given time (1988, 71). Of chief importance in the present context, the claimed *ineffability* of qualia may be reformulatable in terms of the pips' informational richness.[7] Just as in the Jello box example, at first "[t]he only *readily available* way of saying what property M is is just to point to our M-detector and say that M is the shape property detected by this thing here" (1988, 69), when you first hear that E-natural guitar tone your only readily available way of saying what the content of your perceptual state is—i.e., what property it detects—is just to "point" to the state and say that it detects whatever it detects. The informational fecundity of the state might then give rise to judgments to the effect that the content of your conscious experience of the tone is ineffable. Although Dennett is not explicit on this score, I take it that such judgments of ineffability are either relatively isolated, like the presentiments and premonitions of his earlier works, or else are indicative of judgments whose enunciation awaits your mastery of further vocabulary (see again §7.1 above). Or perhaps your pips are chock-full of so much information that they give rise to a barrage of judgments, each clamoring for explicit expression; it might take you some time to give voice to them all, thus lending an impression of ineffability.

Be the details as they may, any such speechlessness is merely "practical": given sufficient time and language mastery, you could provide an exhaustive report of the contents of your conscious perception of that guitar tone:

> Pluck the bass or low E string open and listen carefully to the sound . . . . Now pluck the open string again and carefully bring a finger down lightly over the octave fret to create a high 'harmonic'. Suddenly a new sound is heard: 'purer' somehow and of course an octave higher . . . . But then on a third open plucking one can hear, with surprising distinctness, the harmonic overtone that was isolated in the second plucking. The homogeneity and ineffability of the first experience is gone, replaced by a duality as . . . clearly describable as that of any chord . . . . *There is nothing to stop further refinement of one's capacity to describe this heretofore ineffable complexity* (1988, 71–72; my emphasis).

Indeed, not only will you be able to report that you are hearing an E-natural guitar tone; the implication seems to be that, eventually, you will even be able to report that you are hearing a tone of a certain *determinate* pitch, timbre, loudness, and so forth.

7.3 Attack of the Nuances

There is at least a superficial plausibility to the idea that one's conscious awareness of a (putative) duck/rabbit image just *consists in* having the judgment or thought 'Now it looks like a duck, now like a rabbit'. Or anyway, given the dismal prospects for a phenomenology as tradition-ally conceived, the allure of such a proposal is evident. Returning to the musical realm, let us grant the same with respect to one's conscious awareness of the content of one's structural description of a piece of tonal music. We have acknowledged that the latter kind of content is in principle exhaustively reportable (cf. §2.5); and it seems a short step from there to the stronger constitutive claim. That is, it seems a short step from there to the claim that conscious awareness of the content of one's structural description just *consists in* a series of judgments to the effect that (say) the piece opens with a dominant seventh chord on the upbeat and then moves to a tonic triad on the downbeat, which is then weakly prolonged, and so on. Or so I am prepared to allow for the sake of discussion. Whether the same can be said of mental image rotations I am not sure (see Cam 1987 in this regard), but I don't propose to worry over that question at the moment since I *am* pretty sure that the same *cannot* be said of the nuance representations of the N-level (among other things); that is to say, the content of the N-level cannot be rendered *in conscious awareness* in propositional form. Let us see where the difficulty arises.

How will Dennett's view treat our conscious awareness of N-pitches and N-intervals? For example, how will it treat our conscious awareness of the *particular determinate N-pitch* of that E-natural guitar tone? Suppose it is an E-natural(23). "Now it sounds like *this*": what is the force of our '*this*' here?[8] To be sure, we can follow up such a protocol statement with others: "Now it sounds like an E-natural," "Now it sounds like a slightly high E-natural," "Now it sounds like an E-natural about a quarter-tone high," and so on. However, given our apparent lack of N-interval schemas, no number of such increasingly refined judgments, nor even the conjunction of them all, will suffice to specify the particular deter-minate E-natural(23) that is the content of our conscious awareness. It is not that awareness will be *blank* where the demonstratives occur; but what will occupy it are just more propositional episodes, more intentions-to-say-that-p, and so the content of our awareness will be only as determinate as those allow.

N.B.: I am not here talking—at least I do not *mean* to be talking—about anything essentially private, or immediately apprehensible, or intrinsic, or *essentially* ineffable. Rather, I am talking about a functionally respectable brand of representational (specifically, sensory-perceptual) content of precisely the quotidian variety borne by Dennett's pips; indeed the meandering profile of the N-level seems a perfect auditory analogue to the jagged edge of the Jello box. And my point is that, *contra* Dennett, there most certainly is something "to stop further refinement of one's capacity to describe" one's experience of these fine-grained nuance values. The limits of our schemas are the limits of our language, and *qua* perceivers we are so designed that the grain of conscious experience will inevitably be finer than that of our schemas, no matter how long, or how diligently, we practice.

7.4 In Which We Consider a Possible Reply by Dennett and Refine Our Attack in Light Thereof

Commenting on an earlier (and substantially different) incarnation of the present chapter,[9] Dennett has suggested that he would respond to my argument from the N-level in the way he recently responded to an objection by Phillip Cam (Cam 1987, Dennett 1987b). Of course I cannot be certain what Dennett would say to my argument as currently formulated; but even so the exchange with Cam is instructive in the present regard.

Cam writes:

> [M]y objection to Dennett's promissory notes is . . . that the phenomenology already makes conscious that which on Dennett's view is yet to be propositionally articulated. When it occurs to the subject that the rotated image would look like *that*, the 'that' would specify something totally phenomenologically contentless if there were no content to back it up. And if one supposes that the phenomenological content which backs it up is something propositional, then that propositional content would already be consciously represented. Yet if mental apprehension takes the form of a promissory note, no such content is as yet consciously represented. So there is an excess of phenomenology still to be accounted for here once the propositional content has run dry (338).

I think Cam has mistaken the nature of the promissory notes. The promise is to get the *words* in order, not the judgments (propositional contents). Consider: "When it comes to the judgments about the rotating images the words are still harder to get in order, but it is to the execution of that task that our 'this' and 'that' are promissory notes" (Dennett 1979, 106; see §7.1 above). As I read Dennett, the "phenomenological" content in question is *not* "yet to be propositionally articulated"; rather, it is (already) propositional content that is yet to be *sententially* articulated in the natural language. (Indeed, the idea of issuing a promissory note for future *judgments* or *thoughts*—'I promise to think that P'?—seems a bit of a stretch even for Dennett.) His reply to Cam appears to confirm my interpretation here:

> I see that I was wrong to put any importance on the possibility-in-principle of getting *all* the "content" in an introspective judgment "expressed" (or "explicit") in a sentence. . . . [A]s I have more recently argued ("Beyond Belief," 1982), there is no uniform and problem-free understanding of the relation between propositions (the abstract entities taken traditionally as the "objects" of "propositional" attitudes) and sentences (of English or any other natural language). You can't put into English the most "propositional" (least "imagistic") of "propositional attitudes" without risk of loss or distortion, so it should not surprise or dismay me that there is a difficulty in finding an intuitively adequate sentence to express an introspective judgment about the nature of one's putative mental images (1987, 337).

Dennett here appears to allow that the contents of conscious awareness, *although propositional* or judgmental, may not be expressible in the natural language. The latter claim is something new for Dennett, of course. In discussing some of his earlier works, I suggested that demonstrative promissory notes might be required in cases where, say, consciousness is overcrowded with judgments, or where one has not yet mastered the vocabulary required for exhaustive report. But apart from such merely "contingent" obstacles, the idea had been that "our actual utterances [could not] fail to be expressions of the content of our semantic intentions, [could not] fail to do justice to the access we have to our own inner lives" (1978, 171). In his reply to Cam, however, Dennett introduces the stricter brand of ineffability described above. On what ground does he now suppose that the *propositional* content of conscious awareness might refuse transcription in the natural language?

"Beyond Belief" (1982a) is a dense and lengthy discourse on the often strained relations among psychological states, propositions, and sentences *inter alia*. I *presume* that, alluding to it in the passage cited above, Dennett has in mind certain considerations having to do with the idiosyncratic and perspectival nature of psychological contents. Consider for example the case of Mike, who has "a thing about redheads" (1987a, 148). Roughly, Mike has a negative conception of redheads that influences his attitudes and behavior toward them in various systematic ways. Perhaps, we are asked to suppose, Mike has a certain "bit of cognitive machinery" that is activated whenever redheads are discussed and that disposes him to be suspicious of redheads, to engage in hostile behavior toward redheads, to spread nasty rumors about redheads, and so forth. Suppose furthermore that we have complete knowledge of the functional role played by this bit of cognitive machinery, this thing about redheads, in Mike's mental life—that is, that we have complete knowledge of its place in the causal nexus of his sensory inputs, other mental states, and behavioral outputs. Still, Dennett insists, we might be unable to find a sentence of any natural language that provides an intuitively adequate expression of its content:

> The contribution of Mike's thing about redheads could be perfectly determinate and also undeniably contentful and yet no linguification of it could be more than a mnemonic label for its role. In such a case we could say, as there is often reason to do, that various beliefs are *implicit* in the system. For instance, the belief that redheads are untrustworthy. Or should it be the belief that most redheads are untrustworthy; or "all the redheads I have met"? Or should it be "$(x)(x$ is a redhead $\rightarrow$ the probability is 0.9 that x is untrustworthy)"? The concern with the proper form of the sentence is idle when the sentence is only part of a stab at capturing the implicit content of some nonsentential bit of machinery (1987a, 148-149).

Dennett's point in the reply to Cam, then, must be that just as the content of Mike's thing about redheads may be entirely propositional or judgmental and yet "defy sententialist interpretation" (1987a, 148), so too the contents of the judgments that constitute our conscious awareness. These latter are propositional, presumably, insofar as they are judgments to the effect *that things are a certain way*; it's just that *the way things are* cannot be stated (or stated precisely) in any natural language sentence. If that is so, then the sometime impossibility of explicitly "linguifying" the content of conscious awareness need not raise the dreaded spectre of a phenomenology.

In the pair of passages cited above, Dennett is silent on the issue of representational format. However, in subsequent passages of the reply to Cam, he reaffirms a line familiar from his earlier writings:

> [Furthermore,] I was wrong to think I needed . . . an escape to sentences to preserve my view about the unprivileged . . . access we might have to anything worth calling an image. All I needed was a distinction between images and judgments about images . . . . It is tempting to suppose [that when you look at an image you have drawn on a piece of paper,] there is another image, a private, subjective image in between the public image on the page and your various interpretive judgments about that public image. And there may well be . . . . But your judgments about that inner image are no more privileged than judgments about the public image—and your authorial privilege to stipulate an interpretation of the public image is no less secure than your privilege to stipulate an interpretation of your private images. *Interpretations aren't images,* however (1987b, 339-341; my emphasis).[10]

The distinction between an image and an *interpretation* or *interpretive judgment* is presumably a distinction in format. Hence whatever the format of our conscious judgments or "interpretations" may be, it is not *presentational* (/*analogue*/*imagistic*/*isomorphic*) in any sense that would threaten to reinstate a phenomenology. If imagistic or otherwise "nonpropositional" data structures are involved (as Dennett allows they may be), they lie buried far beneath the conscious surface.

I have discussed the reply to Cam at some length because I want to emphasize that, whatever we think of Dennett's appeal to the short-comings of natural language expressions of psychological content,[11] he cannot respond in *that* way to our argument from the N-level. In other words, he cannot deflect our criticism by asserting that, for reasons analogous (or, for that matter, disanalogous) to those cited in the case of Mike, there may be "a difficulty in finding an intuitively adequate" natural language vocabulary in which to express the conscious content of the N-level. Just for example, recall the numerical N-pitch names 'A-natural(1)', 'A-natural(12)', 'B-flat(17)', and so forth introduced in preceding chapters; these could serve perfectly well for enunciating the content in question. On the contrary, the ineffability of the content of the nuance representations derives not from the absence of terminology adequate to its verbal expression, but rather from the psychological impossibility of *applying* any such terms "by introspection." We cannot report the content of the N-level even in the manner that we can report the content of the mental score; and names for the nuance representations would not be relevantly different in kind from the names we assign to the C-pitch representations.

Consideration of a possible rift between conscious judgment and its explicit report brings our argument from the N-level more sharply into focus. Our claim is not merely that the contents of the nuance representations elude verbal report; we contend furthermore that those contents cannot be rendered *in conscious awareness* in a propositional format.[12] Consider again your perception of that E-natural(23) guitar tone discussed above. There the content to which you have conscious access is sensory-perceptual content; in other words, it is a specification of *how that N-pitch sounds*. Now your mental representation of the E-natural(23) must carry that content, for you in conscious awareness, independently of any *memory* of how that N-pitch sounds. (Recall the revelation of §5.1: for all intents and purposes, we have no memory—or at least no "personally accessible" memory—for nuance values.) And then the problem is that it's hard to see how a "propositional" representation could pull that off: in order to carry such content for you in conscious awareness, a propositional representation would need to link up somehow with the requisite *sensory-perceptual* information in long-term memory; in other words, it would need to link up with an enduring representation of *how the E-natural(23) sounds* (in, say, the manner of Anderson's schematic network). Wouldn't it?

Perhaps an analogy will help here. Suppose you wanted to convey to another listener the determinate N-pitch of that guitar tone (or, if you prefer, the determinate shade of some object); in other words, you wanted to convey to him *how the E-natural(23) sounds*. (Again, he does not, indeed cannot, have any memory of how it sounds). How would you accomplish this? So far as I can see, your only option would be to show him, to *present* him with an instance of an E-natural(23); there would be no *telling* him how it sounds. What I want to suggest is that an analogous challenge confronts your auditory processor in its effort to "convey" to conscious awareness—to convey to *you*—how that E-natural(23) sounds. So far as I can see—and I don't know a less metaphorical or misleading way to say this—your processor must somehow *present* the E-natural(23) to conscious awareness. Absent the long-term schematic storage of "propositional" structures together with the relevant sensory-perceptual information, what other means could there be? (Not to raise false hopes—I have no story to tell about how such presentation might be accomplished. As I warned at the outset, my project here is largely a negative one.). My thought, then, is that the same memory limitation underlies both the ineffability of the nuance representations (i.e., the psychological impossibility of reporting their contents), on the one hand, and the "nonpropositionality" of their format in conscious awareness, on the other.

Harking back to a proposal first mooted in §5.2, one might suppose that your conscious awareness of the E-natural(23) could consist in a cluster of comparative judgments discriminating it from other N-pitch standards. The comparisons would have to be performed in imagination, as it were; for if they required the actual sounding of standard tones, then the content of your conscious awareness of the E-natural(23) would not be fully determinate until all of the relevant standards had been sounded and comparisons made; that is to say, the content of your episode of awareness of the E-natural(23) would not be determinate at the time of its occurrence. But the content of that episode *is* determinate at the time of its occurrence: you are at that moment consciously aware of a particular determinate N-pitch. (Similarly, when looking at an object, you are consciously aware of its particular determinate shade.) Therefore the requisite comparisons would have to be performed (simultaneously?) in imagination. *Then*, even supposing such comparisons are possible, the trouble is that on the proposed view, the contents of your imaginational representations of the relevant N-pitch standards could themselves be specified in conscious awareness only by further comparative judgments; and so on, *ad infinitum*. In short, the contents of such comparative judgments could never be specified; hence the content of your conscious awareness of the E-natural(23) of that guitar tone could never be specified thereby.

Perhaps Dennett would respond here by pointing out the obvious difference between image rotation and nuance perception—viz., that the latter, unlike the former, is veridical perception of an external physical stimulus. Specifically, he might argue that the demonstratives in our protocol statements expressing our conscious awareness of nuances ("Now it sounds like *that*") refer not to any inner items, representational or otherwise, but rather to properties of the causative acoustic stimuli. It is hard to see how this response could serve Dennett's purposes, however. In the present instance the relevant acoustic properties would be frequency (for the N-pitches) and frequency ratio (for the N-intervals); and the difficulty, now familiar from preceding chapters, is that tokens of any given frequency (/frequency ratio) can be heard as instantiating many different N-pitch (/N-interval) types, depending on such factors as the age, health, alertness, and brute resolving power of the listening subject, as well as the acoustical environment and, most importantly, the musical context in which the stimuli are presented. Consequently, reference to an acoustic event of a certain frequency or frequency ratio could not serve to (exhaustively) express the determinate content of our conscious awareness of any N-pitch or N-interval.

7.5 A New Reformulation

What, finally, am I saying? My intention is not to cast a vote for a phenomenology as traditionally conceived, but simply to set out some reasons for doubting that its swansong will go quite as Dennett has written it. Indeed, I suspect that Dennett's proposed "reformulation" of qualia in terms of informational (representational) properties of sense-perceptions looks in just the right place for solutions to some of the puzzles about conscious awareness that have stymied us for so long. Granted, I have urged that at least some of the content of conscious perceptual experience cannot be propositional in form (whatever exactly that comes to), and this conclusion leaves unresolved certain difficulties that his program is designed to eradicate. Nevertheless, in closing let me urge that we take on these difficulties in the interest of developing a picture of conscious experience that follows in the footsteps of Dennett's eliminativist approach while affording a more satisfying reformulation of qualia. Specifically, I want to suggest that the nuance representations of the N-level are (at least part of) the psychological "reality" that inspires, and to that extent explains, our phenomenological rhapsodies. On this supposition, a first go at reformulating qualia might proceed as follows. (I shall take the N-pitch and N-interval representations as my exemplars here, but of course the hope is that analogous claims will be true of other perceptual dimensions as well.)

In the first place, that qualia have been thought *immediately apprehensible* would hardly be surprising given the "location" of the nuance representations in the auditory processing chain: the N-level, recall, is presumably the shallowest level of representation of the musical signal to which the listener has conscious access. Thus *as far as consciousness is concerned*, the nuance representations arrive unheralded, as if from nowhere; in other words, there is no "prior" (viz., shallower) level of representation from which consciousness can regard the N-level as constructed or inferred (as it can, for example, in the case of the mental score). The N-level is, as it were, basic. Our talk of the *atomicity* of qualia may be traceable to this source as well: the determinate pitches and intervals we hear are, after all, the "smallest" values descried along their respective perceptual dimensions.

Second, if the nuance representations of the N-level don't activate N-interval schemas (and we are pretty sure they don't), then they don't get type-identified; that is, they don't get identified as representations of this or that particular N-pitch or N-interval. And if they don't get type-identified, then *to that extent* there is nothing for us to be mistaken about. Of course we can perfectly well type-identify them as E-natural representations (/perceptions/experiences), or as slightly-high-E-natural representations, or as higher-than-the-preceding-E-natural representations, and so forth; and so we can perfectly well be mistaken about any of that. Moreover, if we could further identify them as, say, E-natural(23) representations, then we could be mistaken about their *nuance* types as well. But as is now familiar, we are apparently incapable of any such fine-grained identifications, and so the possibility of error does not arise. Small wonder, then, if our "qualia" talk is inspired by features of the nuance representations, that we should have thought ourselves possessed of *incorrigible access* to our qualia. Crudely: we can't be corrected because we can't be mistaken.

Third, qualia are often said to be *unanalyzable*. Perhaps this feature can find a plausible reformulation in terms of the absence of any systematic structural organization among the nuances. Not that the latter are *meaningless*, of course; as I have repeatedly observed, many nuances in a performance are highly meaningful indicators of a performer's interpretation of a musical work. My point, rather, is that the N-pitches and N-intervals as such do not sustain *among themselves* a system of structural relations anything like that evinced by their chromatic counterparts. At any given point in a tonal work, each of the twelve C-pitches plays (at least) one of twelve functional roles and sustains a corresponding set of structural relationships to its eleven siblings, all depending upon the tonal context currently in effect. More to the point, at any given time each C-pitch (and hence each C-interval) instantiates a variety of structural properties that are manifest *in its sound*: for example, *ceteris paribus* in the key of C major an F-natural (the subdominant) *sounds* relatively unstable, *sounds* like it should progress to G-natural (the dominant), *sounds* like it threatens the primacy of C-natural (the tonic), and so forth. In short, in a well-defined tonal context, C-pitches and C-intervals are anything but unanalyzable. The structural significance of the nuances, on the other hand, derives entirely from the C-pitch and C-interval categories to which they belong; in other words, a nuance is structurally significant only in its role as a value within a certain C-pitch or C-interval category. My thought, then, is that this asymmetry may help to explain the intuition that our qualia are "simple" or "unanalyzable": if features of our nuance representations constitute the reality underlying our talk about qualia, then the intuition that the latter are unanalyzable may owe to the absence of psychologically salient organization among the former.

Lastly, and briefly, in light of the arguments of preceding chapters, a reformulation of the reputed *ineffability* of qualia as the ineffability of the content of the N-level seems entirely natural. Such a view also dovetails nicely with Dennett's own reformulation of the supposed *privacy* of qualia:

> If I wonder whether your blue is my blue, your middle C is my middle C, I can coherently be wondering whether our discrimination profiles over a wide variation in conditions will be approximately the same. And they may not be; people experience the world

quite differently. . . . That idiosyncrasy is the extent of our privacy (1988, 69).

I observed in §5.2 that the "idiosyncrasies" of the pitch and interval discrimination profiles of different listeners would only increase the extent to which the contents of their respective N-levels are ineffable: insofar as discrimination profiles differ intersubjectively, even *ostending* a performance will not guarantee the communication of one's knowledge of its nuances. Accordingly, if those idiosyncrasies (wholly or partly) constitute the privacy of our perceptual experience, we get the attractive result that the privacy of our experience is partly responsible for its ineffability. Who would have thought otherwise?

Of course the foregoing are but hints in the direction a thorough "reformulation" of qualia might take, and a great deal more will need to be said. However that story is ultimately told, my aim in this chapter has been to show that our conscious perception of musical nuances raises the possibility of representation-based, as opposed to qualia-based, objections to Dennett's propositionalist program. In so doing, I hope to have taken a first step toward applying the fruit of our labor on a problem in the philosophy of art to a central problem in the philosophy of mind.

Notes

Chapter 1

1. In the present context I mean by 'aesthetics' the philosophy of art, by 'aesthetic experience' the experience of artworks.
2. In all fairness, Langer was sensitive to the need for explanation in aesthetic theory and is to that extent exempt from the present criticism. Very roughly, she hypothesized that only music (a "presentational" symbol), and not language (a "discursive" symbol), is structured in the right sorts of ways for symbolizing human feelings:

   > I think every work of art expresses...not feelings and emotions which the artist *has*, but feelings and emotions which the artist *knows*; his *insight* into the nature of sentience, his picture of vital experience, phyɔical and emotive and fantastic. . . . Such knowledge is not expressible in ordinary discourse [because] the forms of feeling and the forms of discursive expression are logically incommensurate. . . . Verbal statement . . . is almost useless for conveying knowledge about the precise character of our affective life (1957, 91).

   Intuitively speaking, music and feelings enjoy a certain "fit" that language and feelings miss; as a result, musical experience affords a knowledge of feelings that refuses verbal expression. Although philosophers of art generally agree that Langer's theory fails to realize its explanatory goals, it turns out to share some important features with the view I propose here; see especially chapter 5.
3. Langer 1942, 1957, and Meyer 1956 are good examples. See note 2 above.
4. I imagine most everyone is familiar with the cognitivist program by now; Fodor 1975, 1981a, and Block 1983, v.2 are bibles. In the present context I shall be taking the notion of contentful mental representation more or less for granted, but see Cummins 1989 for an overview of current controversies. See also policy statement 4 on p. 8.
5. For example, see Bharucha 1984b and also chapters 2 and 4.
6. The turn of phrase is Fodor's (1981a, 26).
7. And those values *must* be genuinely perceptual. For reasons brought to light in chapter 6, Goodman cannot here appeal to the so-called phenomenal qualities of his *The Structure of Appearance* (1966).
8. The slide between talk about the music and talk about its mental representation or "knowledge" is not insignificant; as Lerdahl and Jackendoff will put it, "the piece of music is a mentally constructed entity" (1983, 2). The implications of this claim thread through much of the succeeding discussion; I take it up explicitly in chapter 2.
9. The distinction between perceptual knowledge and propositional or descriptive or "conceptual" knowledge, like the distinction between perception and cognition generally, sustains such varied senses in the philosophical and scientific literature that a word or two of clarification is called for. I mean simply to observe a rough and ready

distinction between a kind of knowledge that would have as a paradigm case knowing what red looks like (in the sense of being able to visually recognize red things as such), or how a tonic triad sounds, on the one hand, and a kind of knowledge that would have as a paradigm case, say, knowing that seven is a prime number, or that Paris is the capital of France, on the other. Nothing essential to my view will be lost should the distinction prove a muddy one. Also, for reasons set forth in chapter 5 below, a distinction between "perceptual" and "descriptive" knowledge crosscuts a distinction between knowledge by acquaintance and knowledge by description; content and etiology must be kept apart.

10. Actually, the theory is applied explicitly to Western tonal concert music, but it will be fairly clear how its application to other musical idioms would go. Or at least to some others: it is not at all obvious what the theory would say about Cage's 4'3", for example; but of course that problem is hardly special to *my* view. See §5.3 for further discussion.

11. The theoretical availability of domain-specific musical processes puts us at considerable advantage not only over our predecessors in the philosophy of music, but perhaps indeed over anyone seeking to "naturalize" a theory of visual art (Gombrich 1960 and Arnheim 1954 are obvious instances). Whereas the philosopher of visual art has at his disposal only psychological theories of vision *in general*, the cognitivist philosopher of music can help himself to structures and processes special to musical audition, as distinct from audition in general. Whether domain-specific mechanisms exist for visual art is of course an empirical question, but their failure thus far to emerge, despite the considerably greater time and energy devoted to theories of seeing than to theories of hearing, casts a long shadow.

12. Parts of this essay originally appeared as "Music Discomposed" by Stanley Cavell, in *Art, Mind, and Religion,* W. H. Capitan and D. D. Merrill, editors. Published in 1967 by the University of Pittsburgh Press. Used by permission of the publisher.

Chapter 2

1. Preliminary statements of Fodor's theory are to be found in *The Language of Thought* (1975) and "How Direct is Visual Perception?" (Fodor and Pylyshyn 1981). Unless otherwise indicated, page citations to Fodor herein refer to Fodor 1983.

2. In fact, transducer outputs typically underdetermine the perceived character of the distal layout (e.g., 68–69).

3. Fodor writes: "On at least one usual understanding[,] transducers are analog systems that take proximal stimulations onto more or less precisely covarying neural signals. Mechanisms of transduction are thus *contrasted* with computational mechanisms: whereas the latter may perform quite complicated, inference-like transformations, the former are supposed . . . to preserve the informational content of their inputs, altering only the format in which the information is displayed" (41).

4. The formal properties of a mental representation are those of its (neural) "shape" properties (like, say, spiking frequency or voltage level) that determine its powers of interaction with other representations in the system. In other words, the formal properties of a mental representation are its functionally relevant shape properties. These are often referred to as 'syntactic' properties, but I shall refrain from that usage of the term so as to avoid any confusion with its special sense in linguistic theory.

5. Specifically, the operations of an input system yield *formulae* in a central *code*. Though I cannot explore the issue here, it is worth noting that some theorists would question the extent to which perceptual data structures can be made explicit in the way Fodor's view would seem to require; see Dennett 1987a, 147–148, and 1978, 90–108, for example.

6. 'Successive' is pretty optimistic here. As Fodor rather wistfully admits, "[i]t would be nice if there proved to be a well-ordering of the interlevels of representation computed by each input system, but nothing in the present discussion depends on assuming that this is so" (133, note 20). Among other things, there is likely to be a lot of parallel processing and (intra-modular) feedback (cf. 132, note 14). See Jackendoff 1987, 239–245 for relevant discussion of the musical case.
7. A somewhat lengthy aside. In simplifying things to distill the points of Fodor's 1983 theory that will be important to us here, I have made it seem that input processing *is* perception, or, more specifically, that the output of input processing is a perception of an object in the world. In fact Fodor wants to deny that:

> We have repeatedly distinguished between what the input systems compute and what the organism (consciously or sub-doxastically) *believes*. Part of the point of this distinction is that input systems, being informationally encapsulated, typically compute representations of the distal layout on the basis of less information about the distal layout than the organism has available. Such representations want correction in light of background knowledge (e.g., information in memory) and of the simultaneous results of input analysis in other domains. . . . Call the process of arriving at such corrected representations "the fixation of perceptual belief" (102). . . . [T]he typical function of central systems is the fixation of belief (perceptual or otherwise) by nondemonstrative inference. Central systems look at what the input systems deliver, and they look at what is in memory, and they use this information to constrain the computation of 'best hypotheses' about what the world is like. These processes are, of course, largely unconscious and very little is known about their operation (104). . . . Input analysis may be informationally encapsulated, but perception surely is not. . . . The point of perception is the fixation of belief (73).

Strictly speaking, then, perception is the business of *central* processing and occurs after the input systems have completed their appointed tasks. The distinction between input processing and perception is of course an important one, but I am going to wave my hands over it here; in the present context, nothing will be lost if we think of the input systems as delivering (conscious) perceptions.
8. It's too bad this is not the place for a discourse on modularity, since the case for modular mechanisms in music perception has considerable pull; indeed, Fodor himself suspects the existence of modules "that detect the melodic or rhythmic structure of acoustic arrays" (47). Assembling evidence from a variety of spheres, Howard Gardner concludes that "the core operations of music do not bear intimate connections to the core operations in other areas; and therefore, music deserves to be considered as an autonomous intellectual realm" (1983, 126). See also Jackendoff 1987, chapter 12.
9. The pitch of a tone is also influenced to some degree by its intensity and waveform *inter alia*, and its loudness by its frequency; but we can ignore those complications here.
10. (My easy identification of pitch-time events with notes risks a serious confusion, but it will do for now; refinement comes in chapter 4.) The terms 'duration' and 'length' are used in different ways by different theorists. I shall take duration to be the psychoacoustic correlate of the "physical" property of temporal extent or length. Whether length is transduced seems to be an open question; on the negative side, Carl Seashore writes that "[s]ensitivity to time differs from sensitivity to pitch, intensity, and timbre in that there is no evidence to show that it depends upon the structure of the ear" (1967, 91). See Jones 1990 for an illuminating discussion of the temporal structure of music.

11. Lerdahl and Jackendoff 1977, 1983, Jackendoff and Lerdahl 1977, 1981, Jackendoff 1987; the authors acknowledge a significant debt to Leonard Bernstein's speculations about a musical grammar in his Norton Lectures, *The Unanswered Question* (1976).

12. There does, however, appear to be a significant formal parallel between phonological (prosodic) structure and the musical time-span reduction; see Lerdahl and Jackendoff 1983, §12.3. See also chapter 3 for discussion of what might be called a "formal" parallel between the linguistic semantics and certain features of conscious musical experience.

13. By 'tonal' is meant Western "classical" music (what jazz players often call "serious music") of roughly the period from Bach to Brahms.

14. *Aspects of the Theory of Syntax* 1965 and *Topics in the Theory of Generative Grammar* 1966; it is chiefly this incarnation of Chomsky's position with which Lerdahl and Jackendoff are occupied. See also note 16.

15. As you might expect, ambiguous sentences receive more than one structural description.

16. Chomskian theory has of course undergone considerable revision since the sixties. Very briefly, the trend has been away from explicitly coded rules and toward a smaller number of more general constraints. No longer conceived as a process of hypothesis formation and testing, language acquisition is now thought to consist in the setting of values of various parameters (sometimes described as the "throwing" of a series of binary "switches") that are wired into the system in very general form. In place of the old phrase structure rules are general schemata that license all sorts of possible trees; a number of "modules" then act essentially as filters to sift out the well-formed trees from the ill-formed. See Chomsky 1986 for details.

17. The Lerdahl-Jackendoff grammar may be contrasted with that of Sundberg and Lindblom 1976 (e.g.), which produces simple Swedish folk tunes. The psychological "grammar" for composition, if such there be, may differ from that for perception, while the rules governing performance may differ still; see Lerdahl 1988 and Palmer 1992 for elaboration.

18. (See Lerdahl and Jackendoff 1983, 333, note 3, however, for a disclaimer.) Lerdahl and Jackendoff make universality and innateness claims similar to the ones Chomsky makes for the linguistic competence, but these are rather more problematic in the musical case and I shall not examine them here; see Lerdahl and Jackendoff 1983, especially 281–3, and also Bharucha and Krumhansl 1983 for discussion.

19. Such a picture, by the way, has eminent precursors in the philosophical literature. For instance, as early as 1938 we find R. G. Collingwood writing the following:

> [The artist's] business is not to produce an emotional effect in an audience, but, for example, to make a tune. This tune is already complete and perfect when it exists merely as a tune in his head, that is, an imaginary tune. . . . [T]he music, the work of art, is not the collection of noises, it is the tune in the composer's head (1938, 140).

In a more recent example, John Booth Davies observes that

> [in answer to] the question 'What makes a tune?', we must . . . reply that people make tunes when they listen to music by exercising certain mental abilities which they possess. Listening to a tune is therefore not a passive process of mere reception, but one of active construction. The ear simply picks up, or receives, the sound signal and thereafter the human mind constructs the tune from this raw material (1978, 82).

20. I do not mean to engage in a gratuitous proliferation of terms. 'Feeling', 'experience', 'hearing', 'perception', 'intuition', 'understanding', and 'knowledge' are used more or less interchangeably in the Lerdahl-Jackendoff text and in the musical literature generally, and we shall encounter all of them at one place or another. *I* shall typically

speak of musical *feelings* and musical *knowledge*, for reasons that emerge in the next chapter.

21. As in the linguistic case, ambiguous strings receive more than one (maximally coherent) structural description; see, e.g., Lerdahl and Jackendoff 1983, 66–67.

     Actually, it is not entirely clear—nor for Lerdahl and Jackendoff's immediate purposes is it especially important—whether musical understanding consists in the unconscious structural analysis of the music or in the conscious experience that results therefrom; in other words, it is not entirely clear whether the unconscious analysis *constitutes* or *brings about* musical understanding. We need not resolve the issue here, but in the next chapter we shall explicitly characterize musical understanding as the conscious experience brought about by the unconscious assignment of musical structure.

22. Each of the four sets of rules is further segregated into well-formedness, preference, formation, and correspondence rules, but for present purposes we can afford to set these taxonomic details aside; see Lerdahl and Jackendoff 1983 and Jackendoff 1987, chapter 11, for elaboration.

23. Schubert, "Morgengruss" (voice and piano). We are told that "[i]n the example, the introduction and strophic repetitions have been omitted. The music is already reduced to the quarter-note level. The voice and piano have been compressed into one; the parentheses in measures 6–7 and 17–19 indicate the timbrally subordinate repetitions for piano alone" (Lerdahl and Jackendoff 1983, 264-265).

24. It is presumably in respect of the local/global dimension that the musical rules are kin to the linguistic phrase structure rules. To some extent, the lower-to-higher ordering of the four types of musical analysis can be seen as analogous to the increasing abstractness of phonological, syntactic, and semantic structure in the L-grammar—but the parallel should not be forced. More on this as we go along.

25. The musical literature is rife with theories of consonance and dissonance—what they are and how they arise. According to one prominent account (credited primarily to Helmholtz [1957] and championed by Bernstein [1976] among others), consonance and dissonance result from relationships among the overtones of juxtaposed pitches. The latter view faces a number of difficulties, however, as Lerdahl and Jackendoff point out (1983, 290–294). *They* explain consonance and dissonance instead in terms of (harmonic) distance from the tonic; on their view, pitches that are relatively close to the tonic (e.g., the third and fifth scale degrees) form relatively consonant intervals with it, while relatively more distant pitches (e.g., the fourth and seventh scale degrees) form relatively more dissonant intervals. Intuitively speaking, consonant intervals sound "smooth," "pleasing," and "stable," while dissonant intervals sound "rough," "clashing," and "unstable."

26. Actually, the structural description captures only the *hierarchical* structural features; nonhierarchical structures, such as thematic-motivic relations, are not represented, although the grammar could easily be augmented to include them. For present purposes, nothing will be lost by our speaking as if the structural description represents all of the structural features of the music, hierarchical and nonhierarchical alike.

27. Lerdahl and Jackendoff's is not the only theory that envisions music perception as involving multiple "levels" or "stages" of analysis; see Narmour 1989 for another example.

28. There are those who would contend that the basic unit of psychological significance in music is considerably larger than the pitch-time event—the phrase, for example. See, for example, Serafine 1983 and Handel 1989, 382.

29. The tentative nature of Jackendoff's processing model should be emphasized (see 1987, 239–245). The data bearing on real-time M-grammatical processing are scant, so any theory is bound to be highly speculative.

30. That is the prolongational reduction read, as it were, *cumulatively*. In other words, the conclusion of music processing—viz. that representation to which the listener has conscious access—should be thought of as including much of the content of shallower levels. (See again §2.1 and also note 7 above.) In this connection it is worth pointing out that some global structures specified by the musical competence model may be too "large scale" to be perceptually real, i.e., too large scale to occur in the output of a perceptual inference. For example, if a global level in the prolongational reduction of a piece specifies just three chords (I–V–I), the question arises as to whether, say, the first is actually *heard* as a weak prolongation of the third. One might reasonably contend that we do not perceive such relationships: they may constitute the structure or the "logic" of the music, and indeed we may be able consciously to *infer* from what we perceive that the entire piece reduces to three chords, but such an inference is not an element of one's auditory experience. Simply put, such a structure may be too global to be *heard*. (See Lerdahl and Jackendoff 1983, 188–191 for discussion of these deep levels of prolongational structure.)
31. See Levinson 1980 for a thoughtful examination of the further conditions required to individuate musical works and their performances.
32. See Lerdahl 1988 on the potential schisms between "compositional" and "listening" grammars; see also Scruton 1987.
33. In the present context a trained listener is just an experienced listener with explicit music-theoretic training; the difference between the two is a merely practical one and poses no threat to the general applicability of my theory.
34. With certain qualifications: for instance, the very largest grouping structures—e.g., development sections, recapitulations, entire movements, entire pieces—are easy to recognize and report. Hence with respect to grouping structure at least, the ineffability I discuss above will reside somewhere *between* the most local and most global levels of analysis. Just which structures are known ineffably, in the sense presently at issue, is of course an empirical question.
35. Keep in mind also that, given the holistic interconnections among the operations of the four rule components, a variation in any one structural aspect is likely to ramify throughout much of the analysis.
36. Parts of this essay originally appeared as "Music Discomposed" by Stanley Cavell, in *Art, Mind, and Religion*, W. H. Capitan and D. D. Merrill, editors. Published in 1967 by the University of Pittsburgh Press. Used by permission of the publisher.

Chapter 3

1. There is, of course, a sense of 'know', as in 'Do you know the Brahms horn trio?', that requires more or less long-term retention of the relevant representation(s). On the view I am suggesting, the on-line structural description of a piece also counts as knowledge acquisition, whether or not its content is retained for any substantial period of time. See chapter 5 below for extended discussion of a species of "occurrent" musical knowledge that *cannot* be retained over time.
2. See again chapter 1, note 9.
3. Trained listeners can certainly acquire recognitional knowledge of *some* global levels of structure from a verbal report thereof. For example, any musician will be able to recognize at least some phrase groupings that are described to him and, of course, the beginnings and endings of movements and pieces. In general, though, listeners are likely to be best at recognizing local structures; see again §2.5.
4. An obvious analogy extends to our knowledge of colors. Trivially, my telling you that a certain object is red affords you knowledge of its color only if you already know what red is—some would say: only if you already possess the concept 'red'. And

possession of the concept 'red' presupposes visual acquaintance with some red things: minimally, to know what red is, you've got to know what red things (normally) look like; and to know what red things look like, you've got to *see* some. I don't propose to argue for these truisms here; for corroboration see Wright 1987, Jackson and Pargetter 1987, and McGinn 1983, for example.

5. Incidentally, there are good reasons to think that such an accomplishment does not proceed via a direct "visual-to-motor" information transfer; rather, intermediate auditory (musical) representations are involved. See Jackendoff 1987, 234–236 for discussion.

6. He continues: "[T]he thing one is listening to, listening for, is *the point* of the piece. And to know its point is to know the answer to a sense of the question 'Why is it as it is?' It *bears explanation*, not perhaps the way tides and depressions do, but the way remarks and actions do" (1967, 84).

7. See Kivy 1990, chapter 4, for a helpful survey and analysis of different meanings of 'meaning' in the philosophical literature on music.

8. Actually, Goodman claims that music expresses the *predicates* 'fragile' and 'heroic'; see 1968, 87, and chapter 6.

9. See Kivy 1990, chapter 9, and 1980 for sustained discussion.

10. See Kraut 1991 for an illuminating compendium of possibilities.

11. Or, more properly, on linguistic or otherwise nonmusical meanings. Of course that much is unhelpful at the moment, since I haven't yet said what musical meaning is. My present point is simply that the musical passages cited above could "depend" for their meanings on, say, photographs or paintings as well as on pieces of language. I thank Barbara Scholz for this observation.

12. To explain how they *produce* them, too, but since in the musical case we are concerned only with understanding, and not with production, that is all I shall be talking about here.

13. In keeping with the Lerdahl-Jackendoff musical analogy, the Horrocks examples are taken from his exposition of the standard Chomskian theory of *Aspects* (1965). Chomskian theory has, of course, undergone considerable revision (see Horrocks and also chapter 2, note 16), but that does not alter the point I am making here.

14. Such sentences contain "gaps"—that is, missing constituents; the first contains a gap between 'spotted' and 'yesterday' (filled at some point in the derivation by 'Harriet'), the second a gap between 'said' and 'were' (filled at some point by 'The Bahamas').

15. Questions about the role of semantic factors as data, as evidence, and as justification for the theoretical postulation of linguistic structure also arise in this connection. I shall not discuss those here, however; to the extent that such questions differ from questions about the *discovery* of linguistic structure, my claim does not address them.

16. The point should not be overstated, however. Mari Riess Jones observes (personal communication) that *artistic* language—viz., the language of poems, novels, scripts, screenplays, libretti, etc.—may indeed provoke experiences having a characteristic and salient phenomenology.

17. Of course, something could play the guiding role without playing the explanatory one; in other words, something could constrain the postulation of musical structure without being that which it is the purpose of the theory to explain. (Limitations on memory and processing capacity are plausible candidates.) However, I am presently interested in things—specifically, our musical feelings—that do play both roles, for it is these, by analogy with the linguistic case, that are plausibly viewed as a quasi-semantics.

18. See Schier 1986 for a similar treatment of our understanding of representational pictures.

19. Again, Collingwood sees ahead:

The noises made by the performers, and heard by the audience, are not the music at all; they are only means by which the audience ... can reconstruct for themselves the imaginary tune that existed in the composer's head. ... [T]he listening which we have to do when we hear the noises made by the musicians is in a way rather like the thinking we have to do when we hear the noises made, for example, by a person lecturing on a scientific subject. We hear the sound of his voice; but what he is doing is not simply to make noises, but to develop a scientific thesis. The noises are meant to assist us in achieving what he assumes to be our purpose in coming to hear him lecture, that is, thinking the same scientific thesis for ourselves. ... [W]e must think of communication not as an 'imparting' of thought by the speaker to the hearer, the speaker somehow planting his thought in the hearer's receptive mind, but as a 'reproduction' of the speaker's thought by the hearer, in virtue of his own active thinking (1938, 140).

20. Peter Kivy has recently made an admirable attempt to inject some taxonomic clarity into the proceedings; see 1990, 175–181.
21. Philosophers disagree as to what an emotion is; see Farrell 1988 for a guided tour of competing positions.
22. I think we should read: "No competent listener can listen to this passage ... " See the remarks quoted from Scruton on p. 58 above.
23. Of course, a venerable tradition in philosophy denies the normativity of feelings (as opposed to emotions) altogether; see Kraut 1986 for discussion.
24. See Dowling & Harwood 1986, chapter 8, and Sloboda 1985, chapter 2, for a survey of relevant studies.
25. For extended treatment of these issues among others, see Higgins 1991.
26. Here and throughout I shall mean by 'acquaintance' simply 'sense perception'; there is nothing privileged or epistemically foundational about it. See chapter 5, especially §5.3, for elaboration.
27. Parts of this essay originally appeared as "Music Discomposed" by Stanley Cavell, in *Art, Mind, and Religion*, W. H. Capitan and D. D. Merrill, editors. Published in 1967 by the University of Pittsburgh Press. Used by permission of the publisher.

Chapter 4

1. Perfect pitch is the ability to identify heard pitches in the absence of such cues as the name of the first pitch, or the key signature, of a musical work; in other words, a listener with perfect pitch can identify pitches *in vacuo*, as it were, in the way the rest of us can identify colors. As we shall see in this chapter, the ordinary trained listener identifies pitches only derivatively from his identifications of *intervals* (pitch distances). To that extent his identifications of pitches are relative; hence the term 'relative pitch'. My ordinary trained listener can be characterized as a listener with good relative pitch.
2. I say 'for all intents and purposes' because the "mental score" of a trained listener without perfect pitch will lack a specification of key signature (among other things) and will typically reflect any mistakes by the performer. For present purposes we can ignore these qualifications.
3. See also Jackendoff 1987, 218 in this regard.
4. Vibrato is the periodic pulsation in pitch that occurs in virtually all sustained vocal and instrumental tones; see, e.g., Seashore 1967, 33–52 for details.
5. See Shackford 1962a,b in this regard. On the (equal-tempered) piano keyboard, 'D-sharp' and 'E-flat' are different names ("enharmonic spellings") for the same note;

in the key of E major, for example, the note is called 'D-sharp', whereas in the key of B-flat it is called 'E-flat'.

6. The uncertainty of an experimental stimulus varies inversely with the degree to which its presence and/or characteristics on any given trial can be predicted by the subject. Uncertainty varies directly with the size of the set (i.e., the number of "alternatives") from which the stimulus is selected. See Watson and Kelly 1981 (especially pp. 44–46) for helpful discussion.

The *semitone* or "half step," the interval between any two consecutive pitches on the piano, is the smallest interval in tonal music. (An *interval* is the distance between two pitches). The intervals employed in Western tonal music are comprised in the 12-note chromatic scale, which divides the octave into twelve equal semitone steps. The chromatic intervals (C-intervals) are the *unison* (the interval spanning 0 semitones), *minor second* (1 semitone), *major second* (2 semitones), *minor third* (3 semitones), *major third* (4 semitones), *perfect fourth* (5 semitones), *tritone* (6 semitones), *perfect fifth* (7 semitones), *minor sixth* (8 semitones), *major sixth* (9 semitones), *minor seventh* (10 semitones), *major seventh* (11 semitones), and *octave* (12 semitones).

7. Of course, in hearing N-intervals we are also hearing N-pitches; intervals are, after all, just the distances between pitches. For an example of N-pitch (as opposed to N-interval) perception, consider that when you hear a violinist playing a C-natural and an F-natural, simultaneously and with vibrato, the perfect fourth (the interval or pitch distance) that you hear does not appear to fluctuate in size or position; rather, each of its constituent tones appears to fluctuate in pitch. (For present purposes I shall envision vibrato as a series of discrete contiguous N-pitches, but of course such a "digital" image is unrealistic. Vibrato is a *continuous* variation in pitch, and so its mental representation is likely to be "analogue" in nature. Nothing essential to my view depends upon the former conception, however.)

8. See e.g. Bharucha 1987a, b for a recent model and Handel 1989, chapter 10, for an overview of the psychological literature.

9. Bharucha writes: "The frequency responses of these [pitch input] units are equally spaced along a logarithmic scale of frequency, and are fixed only relative to each other, underlying the relational nature of pitch memory" (1987b, 510). All things being equal, logarithmic equality ensures perceptual equality; that is to say, logarithmically equal steps between frequencies are *perceived* as being equal in size.

10. Although Shepard and Jordan refer to a continuously variable *physical* signal, claiming that *it* gets mapped into the scalar template, it is reasonable to interpret their claim as applying to the mental representation (specifically, the N-level) of that signal. It is of course the mental representation of a stimulus, not the stimulus *per se*, that activates a schema. Also see again the remarks about vibrato in note 7 above.

11. The steps in a diatonic major scale are as follows: 1–2, whole-tone; 2–3, whole-tone; 3–4, semitone; 4–5, whole-tone; 5–6, whole-tone; 6–7, whole-tone; 7–8, semitone. Thus there are semitone steps between scale degrees 3 and 4, and 7 and 8, and whole-tone steps elsewhere.

12. (I say "like virtually any tonal work" in order to allow for pieces like Terry Riley's *In C*, whose key signature is presumably an *essential* feature.) The salience of the intervallic representation of a melody is manifest in the fact that only the C-intervallic relations, and not the specific C-pitches, of a melody are stored over the long term. (Hence Bharucha's remark about pitch memory in the passage cited in note 9 above; see also Dowling 1978 and Handel 1989, 355–361 for relevant discussion.) As Deutsch (1975) observes, we commonly recognize transposed melodies without recognizing *that* they are transposed.

13. As we saw in Bharucha's model above, the representations ("units") in your C-interval schema are probably linked to representations of chords and keys as well. Conse-

quently you will hear the pitches of a tonal melody as instantiating a variety of functional relationships over and above intervallic ones. In the interest of simplicity I abstract from those here.

14. See Repp 1984 for an extensive survey of the literature on categorical perception. Handel 1989, chapter 9, provides a good introduction to the musical case.

15. See, e.g., Burns and Ward 1978. Stimuli in the latter study were pairs of melodic(i.e., successive) intervals, each consisting of two 500-msec sinusoids separated by a 200-msec silence, with an interstimulus interval (ISI) of 1 sec. Thus subjects heard two 500-msec tones with a 200-msec silence between them, then a silence of 1 sec, and then two more 500-msec tones with a 200-msec silence between them; their task was to say whether the two intervals were same or different in width. Halpern and Zatorre 1979 reports similar results for harmonic (i.e., simultaneous) intervals.

    Regarding the issue of stimulus uncertainty, Burns and Ward write:

> The results of these studies show quite conclusively that, when equivalent procedures are used, the perception of melodic musical intervals is equivalent to the perception of stop consonants. Specifically, when equal-step-size discrimination tasks are used, musical intervals are perceived categorically, whereas when variable-step-size discrimination tasks are employed, categorical perception can be eliminated with moderate training. . . . It is tentatively concluded that categorical perception in the case of musical intervals is related to the degree of stimulus uncertainty associated with the procedures used (1978, 466).

Roughly, in the *equal-step-size* discrimination task, the pair of intervals to be discriminated on any given trial was chosen at random from a specified set; whereas in the *variable-step-size* or *adaptive* discrimination task, the pair of intervals to be discriminated on any given trial could be predicted, by the subject, on the basis of feedback about his performance on the preceding trial. Hence stimulus uncertainty, and therewith the likelihood of categorical perception, was greater in the former condition.

16. In addition, whereas the experimental stimuli are typically synthetic sine tones, the overtone complexity of vocal and instrumental tones supplies the listener with acoustic information that may considerably enhance his ability to detect within-category differences along various musical dimensions; see, e.g., Bharucha and Stoeckig 1987 and Bharucha 1987a for relevant discussion.

17. See Wapnick, Bourassa, and Sampson 1982 for further corroboration.

18. The tasks I have in mind are minimal uncertainty 2I-2AFC discrimination tasks and repeated adjustment identification tasks; see Burns and Ward 1982, 254 for discussion.

19. Also, see Ramsey et al. (1991) for a lucid discussion of the differences between so-called classical computational theories like Anderson's and certain more recent connectionist models. As I indicated in chapter 1, however, the account of musical ineffability proposed here will stand or fall independently of the outcome of that particular paradigm clash.

20. See, e.g., Deutsch 1969 and Dowling 1978 for relevant discussion.

Chapter 5

1. See also Dowling 1978, Balzano 1980, and Shepard 1982 in this connection.

2. Incidentally, those familiar with Paul Churchland's eliminative materialism (cf. especially 1985) may be interested to discover that our apparent lack of N-interval schemas suggests that we could not replace our current folk psychological sensation reports by talk about, say, neural spiking frequencies—at least not in any sense amounting to more than a mere terminological shift. Differences among spiking rates would have to be at least as fine-grained as the differences we (consciously) hear among nuances, and hence are equally unlikely to be "schematizable." (The 1984

Shepard and Jordan study discussed in §4.2 also indicates that perceptual processes may be far less cognitively penetrable than Churchland seems to think.) At a minimum, the sort of revision Churchland has in mind would need to supplant the commonsense framework with talk about a schematizable (probably more abstract) neurophysiological property.

3. Ivan Fox is the sensitive and careful reader who put the question to me in this way.

4. The nonstructural features of a musical performance are those of its audible features whose representations are delivered to consciousness but not represented in the structural description. The nuances are the finest within-category values we can discriminate (the "determinates") along the various audible dimensions of a performance. The two classes of features may or may not be coextensive, but nothing in my story turns on that either way; all it requires is that the nuances be nonstructural.

5. I am exaggerating just a little here. In fact, there is evidence to suggest that listeners can remember at least some nuances for very short periods; for example, Konig (1957) reports that listeners were able to discriminate tones differing in pitch by a sixteenth-tone even with an ISI (interstimulus interval) as long as 10 sec. Strictly speaking, then, I should say that *for all intents and purposes* the only way to know the music is to be hearing it.

6. Of course, performances are plausibly regarded as works of art in their own right; indeed I shall endorse such a view in the next section. But the present point is, I take it, clear enough.

7. The idea is neither peculiar to, nor original with, Cavell. Just for example, David Prall writes that

> aesthetic experience is an experience of an object as apprehended delightfully, primarily too, as so apprehended directly through the senses. That is what is properly signified by the term aesthetic [sic] in the first place, and it is the primary meaning, never to be neglected in the analysis of aesthetic experience (1967, 19).

Indeed the idea that an artwork could be known *independently* of sense perception is probably the exception to, rather than the rule in, the philosophical literature.

8. Not to deny the obvious disanalogy between music and language: musical works, unlike linguistic ones, *are* addressed to a particular sensory modality.

9. Consider for example the following passage from Prall:

> [A]esthetic experience ... is, no matter how much of ourselves it involves, the experience of the surface of our world directly apprehended, and this surface is always, it would seem, to some degree pleasant or unpleasant to sense in immediate perception. But the use of the word perception here may too strongly suggest more than any immediacy. An act of perception may look beyond the surface and fill in our immediate data with the content of previous perceptions or similar ones. We may perceive solidity through a mere surface area, a substantial round orange where for bare sense apprehension there is perhaps only a spot of orange color. Of the delight that is apprehended beauty it is better to say not that it is perceived but that it is intuited. For it is characteristic of aesthetic apprehension that the surface fully present to sense is the total object of apprehension. We do not so much perceive an object as intuit its appearance, and as we leave this surface in our attention, to go deeper into meanings or more broadly into connections and relations, we depart from the typically aesthetic attitude (1967, 20).

10. Indeed, the inclination to say that "something is missing" from electronically synthesized renditions of the concert literature may owe in part to their relative lack of nuance. Recent developments in musical software, however, may render such criticisms a thing of the past.

11. Parts of this essay originally appeared as "Music Discomposed" by Stanley Cavell, in *Art, Mind, and Religion*, W. H. Capitan and D. D. Merrill, editors. Published in 1967 by the University of Pittsburgh Press. Used by permission of the publisher.

Chapter 6

1. Unless otherwise indicated, page numbers in parentheses in the text refer to *Languages of Art* (1968).
2. A symbol *scheme* is a class of syntactic characters or types; add a semantics and you have a symbol *system*. I shall help myself to talk of syntactic *types* and *tokens*, though Goodman would surely disapprove; see, e.g., 131, n. 3.
3. Objects *comply* with the symbols that *denote* them (143–144).
4. We are told that "'[t]heoretically possible' may be interpreted in any reasonable way; whatever the choice, all logically and mathematically grounded impossibility . . . will of course be excluded" (136).
5. After completing the present discussion I have discovered that Kendall Walton (1971) noticed the same error in the Goodman text some time ago. Walton reformulates (3) in this somewhat weaker way: "For every character K and every mark m, determination either that m does not belong to K or that m belongs either to K or to no character is theoretically possible" (85). Various considerations can be brought to bear for and against either of the two reformulations (Walton's and mine), but I don't propose to worry about those here. On the untendentious assumption that every mark belongs to one and only one character, Walton's reformulation comes to the same as mine in any case.
6. Goodman would include speeds as tokens of the *metronomic* types '60 mm', '88 mm', etc. (185–186), and key ought to enter in as well, but for simplicity's sake we can ignore those features here.
7. Among the exceptions are figured bass and free cadenza markings; see 1968, 183–184.
8. Though most of the supplementary markings are syntactically dense, most of them are not also syntactically undifferentiated; hence taken by themselves, as it were, they generate no ineffability. The ineffability results rather from their (undeterminable) relationship to their respective compliance-classes.
9. Goodman writes: "If we consider piano scores alone, the language is highly redundant since, for example, the same *sound-events* comply with the characters for c-sharp, d-flat, e-triple-flat, b-double-sharp, and so on....In a violin score the characters for c-sharp and d-flat have no compliants in common" (181–182; my emphasis). He then adds in a footnote that "[t]his may be disputed. I am told that a tone of, say, 333 vibrations per second is accepted for either character" (182). '333 vibrations per second' is a specification of acoustic frequency.
10. Actually, indefatigable nominalist that he is, Goodman defines exemplification in the following way: A symbol S exemplifies a *label* P if and only if P applies to S and S refers to P. So a red tailor's swatch, for instance, exemplifies the *predicate* 'red', not the property *red* (54–55). Given the awkwardness of this way of talking, and the fact that Goodman himself frequently slips into talk of properties, we need have no qualms about employing the formulation in the text above.
11. Inverted because of the direction of reference from performance "up" to exemplified property. (In the cited passage, Goodman's talk of performances "taken as sound-events" should be replaced by talk of performances taken as sequences of nuances. Or so I contend.)
12. Of course, we have claimed that the nuance ineffability attends our *knowledge* of musical performances. I am not certain what Goodman would make of our usage of 'know', but in any case that does nothing to threaten the fundamental kinship between

his theory of ineffability and ours: on both views, one perceives—i.e., is perceptually acquainted with—certain musical values (pitches, interval widths, dynamics, etc.) but cannot identify, hence cannot say, which values they are.

13. I am indebted to Lee Brown for helpful discussion of the material presented in this section. See Margolis 1981 for a lucid exposure of some of the difficulties afflicting Goodman's exemplification relation.

14. This proposal is inspired by the discussion of phenomenal qualities in Goodman's *The Structure of Appearance* (1966), sections IX and X.

15. I thank Barbara Scholz for posing this question.

16. Indeed, even if the recognition of N-pitches as such didn't require schemas of the sort we actually employ, that recognition *by itself* would constitute a major transfiguration of musical experience. As long as the N-pitches are being recognized (type-identified) as such, one might contend, they are not being heard *as* nuances within the C-pitch categories.

Chapter 7

1. See, for example, Dennett 1978, 1979, 1982, 1988. Dennett's latest *magnum opus*, *Consciousness Explained* (1991), appeared as the present work was nearing completion, and the exigencies of my own publication schedule preclude any explicit treatment of it here. If Dennett either now endorses, or has at other times endorsed, a position different from the one ascribed to him above, then my present criticisms do not touch it.

2. Dennett (especially 1988, 1991), Paul Churchland (e.g., 1985), and Patricia Kitcher (e.g. 1979) are noteworthy among the pessimists. But see Fox 1989 for an admirable attempt to carve out a coherent phenomenology.

3. Quotations from Dennett 1979 reprinted by permission of Kluwer Academic Publishers.

4. Of course there is no hiding the fast and loose play here with two notoriously slippery distinctions—that between "form" (format) and "content," on the one hand, and that between "propositional" and "presentational" formats, on the other. Since a thorough analysis of these distinctions would require a book in itself, I shall for present purposes follow Dennett in relying on a more or less intuitive grasp (along with some well-placed examples) of the notions at issue. The reader interested in formats of representation, mental and otherwise, will want to have a look at Goodman 1968, Dretske 1981, Haugeland 1982, Block 1981, Kosslyn 1980, and Kosslyn et al. 1977, for starters.

5. "'quine, v. To deny resolutely the existence or importance of something real or significant'" (Dennett 1988, 42). The title 'Quining Qualia' is thus an ironic one.

6. It may be that I misread Dennett here. Whereas I have taken conscious awareness, in the manner of Dennett's earlier writings, to consist in a series of (occurrent) judgments or propositional episodes ("acts of re-identification and recognition"), he may instead be urging that awareness consists in the disposition to make such judgments. That is to say, his thought may be that being conscious consists in being in a state whose pips have the "power to provoke" such judgments. Insofar as a dispositional reading of the passage at issue is correct, my arguments here do not touch it. I think there is evidence to support both readings; apparently favoring the one I endorse in the text above is (e.g.) Dennett's claim that we "do not have to know how we identify or re-identify or gain access to such internal response types in order to be able so to identify them" (1988, 71). Here, "gaining access" seems to be on a par with identifying and re-identifying, which suggests that occurrent "acts" of gaining access are on a par with "acts" of identification and re-identification. (Here and elsewhere I am indebted to Ivan Fox for helpful discussion.)

7. N.B.: These "reformulations" are not identity claims; Dennett is an eliminativist about qualia. His proposals are best viewed as hypotheses about the psychological or neural "reality" that (on his view) inspires certain natural but wrongheaded ways of thinking and talking about conscious experience.

8. Of course, in the image rotation case, the 'it' of our protocol statements ostensibly refers to an "internal" object of some kind, whereas the 'it' here is plausibly interpreted as referring to an "external" object (viz. an acoustic signal). The disparity is immaterial in the present connection, however, since the signal's sounding a certain way (sounding "like *this*") just is a matter of its being mentally represented in a certain way. In other words, whether the protocol statement in question is framed as a statement about internal representations or about external stimuli, what's at issue in both cases is the (conscious) content of a mental representation. (See §7.4 though, for a proposal in which the disparity *is* important.)

9. Session II: "Science of Subjectivity," 15th Annual Meeting, Society for Philosophy and Psychology, Tucson, Arizona (1989).

10. See also Dennett 1978, 161, in this regard.

11. A great deal can be (and has been) said both for and against the claim that the contents of our mental states may "defy sententialist interpretation" in the natural language; see e.g. Baker 1987, Fodor 1987, Burge 1979, 1986, Loar 1988, McGinn 1989 for starters.

12. Despite indications in the passage from Cam that I cite (somewhat self-servingly) above, what really worries him is not, as Dennett seems to think, whether the (propositional) content of awareness can be *sententially* expressed, but rather whether the content of awareness can be rendered in propositional form in the first place: "[W]hatever we make of the likeness between pencil-and-paper images and mental ones, they are forms of representation which have in common features not readily transposed into propositional form" (Cam 1987, 338). If Cam's argument is successful (and I think it probably is), it shows that, contrary to certain assertions by Dennett (cf. Cam 1987, 336–337), the content of awareness *need not* be rendered entirely in propositional form. To pose a serious obstacle to Dennett's program, however, one must show that at least some of the content of awareness *cannot* be rendered entirely in propositional form. It is to the latter goal that my efforts here aspire.

Bibliography

Anderson, J. (1980) *Cognitive Psychology*. San Francisco: W. H. Freeman.

Arnheim, R. (1954) *Art and Visual Perception*. Berkeley: University of California.

Baker, L. R. (1987) *Saving Belief*. Princeton: Princeton University Press.

Balzano, G. J. (1980) The group-theoretic description of twelvefold and microtonal pitch systems. *Computer Music Journal* 4:66-84.

Bell, C. (1914) *Art*. London: Chatto and Windus.

Bernstein, L. (1976) *The Unanswered Question*. Cambridge: Harvard University Press.

Bharucha, J. J. (1984a) Event hierarchies, tonal hierarchies, and assimilation: A reply to Deutsch and Dowling. *Journal of Experimental Psychology* 113:421-425.

Bharucha, J. J. (1984b) Anchoring effects in music: The resolution of dissonance. *Cognitive Psychology* 16:485-518.

Bharucha, J. J. (1987a) Music cognition and perceptual facilitation: A connectionist framework. *Music Perception* 5:1-30.

Bharucha, J. J. (1987b) MUSACT: A connectionist model of musical harmony. *Proceedings of the Cognitive Science Society* . Hillsdale, N.J.: Lawrence Erlbaum, 508-517.

Bharucha, J. J., and Krumhansl, C. (1983) The representation of harmonic structure in music: Hierarchies of stability as a function of context. *Cognition* 13:63-102.

Bharucha, J. J., and Stoeckig, K. (1986) Reaction time and musical expectancy: priming of chords. *Journal of Experimental Psychology: Human Perception and Performance* 12(4):403-410.

Bharucha, J. J., and Stoeckig, K. (1987) Priming of chords: Spreading activation or overlapping frequency spectra?" *Perception and Psychophysics* 47(6):519-524.

Block, N., ed. (1981) *Imagery*. Cambridge: MIT Press/Bradford Books.

Block, N., ed. (1983) *Studies in the Philosophy of Psychology*, vols. 1, 2. Cambridge: MIT Press/Bradford Books.

Burge, T. (1979) Individualism and the mental. In *Studies in Epistemology, Vol. 4, Midwest Studies in Philosophy*, edited by P. French, T. Euhling, and H. Wettstein. Minneapolis: University of Minnesota Press.

Burge, T. (1986) Individualism and psychology. *Philosophical Review* 95(1):3-45.

Burns, E. M., and Ward, W. D. (1977) Categorical perception of musical intervals. *Journal of the Acoustical Society of America* 55, 456(A).

Burns, E. M., and Ward, W. D. (1978) Categorical perception--phenomenon or epiphenomenon: Evidence from experiments in the perception of musical intervals. *Journal of the Acoustical Society of America* 63(2):456-468.

Burns, E. M., and Ward, W. D. (1982) Intervals, scales, and tuning. In Deutsch (ed.) *The Psychology of Music*. New York: Academic Press, 241-269.

Cam, P. (1987) Propositions about images. *Philosophy and Phenomenological Research* 48(2):336-338.

Cavell, S. (1967a) Music Discomposed. In *Art, Mind, and Religion*, edited by W.H. Capitan and D.D. Merrill. Pittsburgh: University of Pittsburgh Press.

Cavell, S. (1967b) Rejoinders. In *Art, Mind, and Religion,* edited by W.H. Capitan and D.D. Merrill. Pittsburgh: University of Pittsburgh Press.

Chomsky, N. (1965) *Aspects of the Theory of Syntax.* Cambridge: MIT Press.

Chomsky, N. (1966) *Topics in the Theory of Generative Grammar.* The Hague: Mouton.

Chomsky, N. (1986) *Knowledge of Language: Its Nature, Origin, and Use.* New York: Praeger.

Churchland, P. (1983) Consciousness: The transmutation of a concept. *Pacific Philosophical Quarterly* 64:80-95.

Churchland, P. (1985) Qualia, reduction, and the direct introspection of brain states. *Journal of Philosophy* 82(1):435-450.

Clarke, E. F. (1987) Levels of structure in the organization of musical time. *Contemporary Music Review* 2:211-238.

Collingwood, R. G. (1938) *The Principles of Art.* Oxford: Oxford University Press.

Cummins, R. (1989) *Meaning and Mental Representation.* Cambridge: MIT Press / Bradford Books.

Davies, J. B. (1978) *The Psychology of Music.* Stanford: Stanford University Press.

Dennett, D. C. (1978) *Brainstorms.* Cambridge: MIT Press / Bradford Books.

Dennett, D. C. (1979) On the absence of phenomenology. In *Body, Mind, and Method,* edited by D. F. Gustavson and B. L. Tapscott. Dordrecht: D. Reidel, 93-114.

Dennett, D. C. (1982) How to study human consciousness empirically—or—nothing comes to mind. *Synthese* 53:159-80.

Dennett, D. C. (1987a) Beyond belief. In *The Intentional Stance.* Cambridge: MIT Press / Bradford Books, 117-212.

Dennett, D. C. (1987b) Commentary on Cam. *Philosophy and Phenomenological Research* 48(2):339-341.

Dennett, D. C. (1988) Quining qualia. In *Consciousness in Contemporary Science,* edited by A. Marcel and E. Bisiach. New York: Oxford University Press, 42-77.

Dennett, D. C. (1991) *Consciousness Explained.* Boston: Little, Brown.

Deutsch, D. (1969) Musical recognition. *Psychological Review* 76:300-307.

Deutsch, D. (1975) The organization of short-term memory for a single acoustic attribute. In *Short-Term Memory,* edited by D. Deutsch and J. A. Deutsch. New York: Academic.

Dewey, J. (1934) *Art as Experience.* New York: Minton.

Dickie, G. (1962) Is psychology relevant to aesthetics? *The Philosophical Review* 71:285-302.

Dowling, W. J. (1978) Scale and contour: Two components of a theory of memory for melodies. *Psychological Review* 88:503-522.

Dowling, W. J., and Harwood, D. L. (1986) *Music Cognition.* New York: Academic Press.

Drake, C., and Palmer, C. (1991) Recovering structure from expression in music performance. *Proceedings of the Cognitive Science Society.* Hillsdale, N.J.: Lawrence Erlbaum, 688-692.

Dretske, F. (1981) *Knowledge and the Flow of Information.* Cambridge: MIT Press / Bradford Books.

Dummett, M. (1975) Wang's paradox. *Synthese* 30:301-324.

Farrell, D. (1988) Recent work on the emotions. *Analyse & Kritik* 10:71-102.

Fodor, J. A. (1975) *The Language of Thought.* Cambridge: Harvard University Press.

Fodor, J. A. (1981) *Representations.* Cambridge: MIT Press / Bradford Books.

Fodor, J. A. (1983) *The Modularity of Mind.* Cambridge: MIT Press / Bradford Books.

Fodor, J. A. (1987) *Psychosemantics.* Cambridge: MIT Press / Bradford Books.

Fodor, J. A. (1990) *A Theory of Content and Other Essays.* Cambridge: MIT Press / Bradford Books.

Fodor, J. A., and Pylyshyn, Z. (1981) How direct is visual perception? An examination of Gibson's 'ecological approach'. *Cognition* 9:193-196.

Fodor, J., and Pylyshyn, Z. (1988) Connectionism and cognitive architecture: A critical analysis. *Cognition* 28:3-71.

Fox, I. (1989) On the nature and cognitive function of phenomenal content—Part one. *Philosophical Topics* 17:81-117.

Gabrielsson, A. (1974) Performance of rhythmic patterns. *Scandinavian Journal of Psychology* 15:63-72.

Gabrielsson, A. (1982) Perception and performance of musical rhythms. In *Music, Mind, and Brain: The Neuropsychology of Music*, edited by M. Clynes. New York: Plenum Press, 159-169.

Gabrielsson, A. (1986) Rhythm in music. In *Rhythm in Psychological, Linguistic and Musical Processes*, edited by J. R. Evans and M. Clynes. Springfield, Illinois: Charles C Thomas, 131-167.

Gardner, H. (1983) *Frames of Mind*. New York: Basic Books.

Gombrich, E. (1960) *Art and Illusion*. New York: Pantheon.

Goodman, N. (1966) *The Structure of Appearance*. Indianapolis: Bobbs-Merrill.

Goodman, N. (1968) *Languages of Art*. Indianapolis: Bobbs-Merrill.

Goodman, N. (1976) Languages of Art. Indianapolis: Hackett Publishing Company.

Halpern, A. R., and Zatorre, R. J. (1979) Identification, discrimination, and selective adaptation of simultaneous musical intervals. *Journal of the Acoustical Society of America* 65:540(A).

Handel, S. (1989) *Listening: An Introduction to the Perception of Auditory Events*. Cambridge: MIT Press/Bradford Books.

Hanslick, E. (1957) *The Beautiful in Music*, translated by Gustav Cohen. Indianapolis: Bobbs-Merrill.

Hardin, C. L. (1988) *Color for Philosophers*. Indianapolis: Hackett Publishing Company.

Haugeland, J. (1982) Analog and analog. In *Mind, Brain, and Function*, edited by J. I. Biro and R. W. Shahan. Norman: University of Oklahoma Press, 213-226.

Helmholtz, H. L. F. (1954) *On the Sensations of Tone*. New York: Dover.

Hevner, K. (1936) Experimental studies of the elements of expression in music. *American Journal of Psychology* 48:248-268.

Higgins, K. M. (1991) *The Music of Our Lives*. Philadelphia: Temple University Press.

Horrocks, G. (1987) *Generative Grammar*. London: Longman Linguistics Library.

Jackendoff, R. (1987) *Consciousness and the Computational Mind*. Cambridge: MIT Press/Bradford Books.

Jackendoff, R., and Lerdahl, F. (1977) Review article: *The Unanswered Question* by Leonard Bernstein. *Language* 53(4):883-894.

Jackendoff, R., and Lerdahl, F. (1981) Generative music theory and its relation to psychology. *Journal of Music Theory* 25(1):45-90.

Jackson, F. (1982) Epiphenomenal qualia. *Philosophical Quarterly* 32:127-132.

Jackson, F. (1986) What Mary didn't know. *The Journal of Philosophy* 83(5):291-295.

Jackson, F., and Pargetter, R. (1987) An objectivist's guide to subjectivism about color. *Revue Internationale de Philosophe* 41(160):126-141.

Jones, M. R. (1990) Musical events and models of musical time. In *Cognitive Models of Time*, edited by R. Block. Hillsdale, N.J.: Lawrence Erlbaum, 207-240.

Jones, M. R., and Halpern, S., eds. (1991) *Cognitive Bases of Musical Communication*. Washington, D.C.: American Psychological Association.

Jones, M. R., and Yee, W. (in press) Attending to auditory events. In *Cognitive Aspects of Human Audition*, edited by S. McAdams. Oxford: Oxford University Press.

Jones, M. R., Boltz, M., and Kidd, G. (1982) Controlled attending as a function of melodic and temporal context. *Perception and Psychophysics* 32:211-218.

Jordan, D. S. (1987) Influence of the diatonic tonal hierarchy at microtonal intervals. *Perception and Psychophysics* 41(6):482-488.

Kant, I. (1968) *Critique of Judgment*, translated by J. H. Bernard. New York: Haffner.

Kennick, W. E. (1967) The ineffable. In *The Encyclopedia of Philosophy*, edited by Edwards 4. New York: Macmillan, 181-183.

Kidd, G., Boltz, M., and Jones, M. R. (1984) Some effects of rhythmic context on melody recognition. *American Journal of Psychology* 97:153-173.

Kitcher, P. (1979) Phenomenal qualities. *American Philosophical Quarterly* 16:123-129.

Kivy, P. (1980) *The Corded Shell: Reflections on Musical Expression*. Princeton: Princeton University Press.

Kivy, P. (1990) *Music Alone*. Ithaca: Cornell University Press.

Konig, E. (1957) Effect of time on pitch discrimination thresholds under several psychophysical procedures; comparison with intensity discrimination thresholds. *Journal of the Acoustical Society of America* 29(5):606-612.

Kosslyn, S. (1980) *Image and Mind*. Cambridge: Harvard University Press.

Kosslyn, S., Murphy, G. L., Bemesderfer, M. E., and Feinstein, K. J. (1977) Category and continuum in mental comparisons. *Journal of Experimental Psychology: General* 106(4).

Kraut, R. (1986) Feelings in context. *Journal of Philosophy* 83(11):642-652.

Kraut, R. (1991) On pluralism and indeterminacy. *Midwest Studies in Philosophy XVI: Philosophy and the Arts*, edited by P. A. French, T. E. Uehling, Jr., and H. K. Wettstein. Notre Dame: University of Notre Dame Press, 209-225.

Kraut, R. (in press) On perceiving the music correctly. In *The Interpretation of Music: Philosophical Essays*, edited by M. Krausz. Oxford: Oxford University Press.

Kuhns, Richard E. (1978) Representation in music. *The British Journal of Aesthetics* 18(1):120-125.

Langer, S. K. (1942) *Philosophy in a New Key: A Study in the Symbolism of Reason, Rite, and Art*. New York: New American Library of World Literature.

Langer, S. K. (1953) *Feeling and Form: A Theory of Art*. New York: Charles Scribner's Sons.

Langer, S. K. (1957) *Problems of Art*. New York: Pantheon.

Lerdahl, F. (1988) Cognitive constraints on compositional systems. In *Generative Processes in Music*, edited by J. Sloboda. Oxford, England: Oxford University Press, 231-259.

Lerdahl, F., and Jackendoff, R. (1977) Toward a formal theory of tonal music. *Journal of Music Theory* 21:111-171.

Lerdahl, F., and Jackendoff, R. (1983) *A Generative Theory of Tonal Music*. Cambridge: MIT Press/Bradford Books.

Levinson, J. (1980) What a musical work is. *The Journal of Philosophy* 77(1):5-28.

Loar, B. (1988) Social content and psychological content. In *Contents of Thought*, edited by R. H. Grimm and D. D. Merrill. Tucson: University of Arizona Press, 99-110.

Margolis, J. (1981) What is when? When is what? Two questions for Nelson Goodman. *Journal of Aesthetics and Art Criticism* 39(3):266-268.

McGinn, C. (1983) *The Subjective View: Secondary Qualities and Indexical Thoughts*. Oxford: Oxford University Press.

McGinn, C. (1989) *Mental Content*. New York: Blackwell.

Meyer, L. S. (1956) *Emotion and Meaning in Music*. Chicago: University of Chicago Press.

Moore, B. C. J. (1977) *Introduction to the Psychology of Hearing*. London: The Macmillan Press Ltd.

Nagel, T. (1974) What is it like to be a bat? Reprinted in *Mortal Questions*. Cambridge: Cambridge University Press, 165-180.

Narmour, E. (1989) The 'genetic code' of melody: Cognitive structures generated by the implication-realization model. *Contemporary Music Review* 4:45-63.

Palmer, C. (1988) *Timing in Skilled Music Performance*. Unpublished doctoral dissertation. Cornell University.

Palmer, C. (1989) Mapping musical thought to musical performance. *Journal of Experimental Psychology: Human Perception and Performance* 15(12):331-346.

Palmer, C. (1992) The role of interpretive preferences in music performance. In Jones and Halpern (eds.), 249-262.

Prall, D. W. (1967) *Aesthetic Judgment*. New York: Crowell.

Raffman, D. (1988) Toward a cognitive theory of musical ineffability. *Review of Metaphysics* 41:685-706.

Raffman, D. (1991) The meaning of music. *Midwest Studies in Philosophy* 16:360-377.

Raffman, D. (in press) Goodman, density, and the limits of sense perception. In *The Interpretation of Music: Philosophical Essays*, edited by M. Krausz. Oxford: Oxford University Press.

Ramsey, W., Stich, S., and Garon, J. (1991) Connectionism, eliminativism, and the future of folk psychology. In *The Future of Folk Psychology*, edited by J. E. Greenwood. Cambridge: Cambridge University Press, 93-119.

Repp, B. (1984) Categorical perception: Issues, methods, and findings. In *Speech and Language*, vol. 10: *Advances in Basic Research and Practice*, edited by N. Lass. Orlando: Academic Press, 224-335.

Schank, R. C., and Abelson, R. (1977) *Scripts, Plans, Goals, and Understanding*. Hillsdale, N.J.: Lawrence Erlbaum.

Schier, F. (1986) *Deeper Into Pictures: An Essay on Pictorial Representation*. New York: Cambridge University Press.

Schopenhauer, A. (1958) *The World as Will and Idea*, translated by R. B. Haldane and J. Kemp. London: Kegan Paul, Trench, and Trubner.

Scruton, R. (1987) Analytical philosophy and the meaning of music. *Journal of Aesthetics and Art Criticism* XLVI:169-176.

Seashore, C. (1967) *The Psychology of Music*. New York: Dover.

Serafine, M.-L. (1983) Cognition in music. *Cognition* 14:119-183.

Shackford, C. (1962a). Some aspects of perception. Part II. *Journal of Music Theory* 6:66-90.

Shackford, C. (1962b). Some aspects of perception. Part III. *Journal of Music Theory* 6:295-303.

Shepard, R. (1982) Geometrical approximations to the structure of musical pitch. *Psychological Review* 89:305-333.

Shepard, R., and Jordan, D. (1984) Auditory illusions demonstrating that tones are assimilated to an internalized musical scale. *Science* 226:1333-1334.

Shepard, R. N., and Metzler, J. (1971) Mental rotation of three-dimensional objects. *Science* 171:701-703.

Siegel, Jane A., and Siegel, W. (1977) Categorical perception of tonal intervals: Musicians can't tell *sharp* from *flat*. *Perception and Psychophysics* 21(5):399-407.

Sloboda, J. (1985) *The Musical Mind: The Cognitive Psychology of Music*. Oxford: Oxford University Press.

Smolensky, P. (1988) On the proper treatment of connectionism. *The Behavioral and Brain Sciences* 11:1-23.

Soames, S., and Perlmutter, D. M. (1979) *Syntactic Argumentation and the Structure of English*. Berkeley and Los Angeles: University of California Press.

Stich, S. (1984) *From Folk Psychology to Cognitive Science: The Case Against Belief*. Cambridge: MIT Press/Bradford Books.

Stravinsky, I. (1942) *The Poetics of Music*. Cambridge: Harvard University Press.

Sundberg, J., and Lindblom, B. (1976) Generative theories in language and music descriptions. *Cognition* 4:99-122.

Ullman, S. (1979) *The Interpretation of Visual Motion*. Cambridge: MIT Press.

Walton, K. (1971) Languages of art: An emendation. *Philosophical Studies* 22(5-6):82-85.

Wapnick, J., Bourassa, G., and Sampson, J. (1982) The reception of tonal intervals in isolation and in melodic context. *Psychomusicology* 2(1):21-36.

Watson, C. S., and Kelly, W. J. (1981) The Role of Stimulus Uncertainty in the Discrimination of Auditory Patterns. In *Auditory and Visual Pattern Recognition*, edited by D. J. Getty and J. N. Howard. Hillsdale, N.J.: Lawrence Erlbaum, 37-59.

Wittgenstein, L. (1958) *Philosophical Investigations*. Oxford: Basil Blackwell.

Wright, C. (1987) Further reflections on the sorites paradox. *Philosophical Topics* 15(1):227-290.

Index

Abelson, R., 68
Activation, spreading of, 70, 81
Aesthetic emotion. *See* Emotions
Anderson, J., 8, 68, 79–81, 140

Bell, C., 56, 60
Bharucha, J. J., 9, 69–70, 76–77, 80
Burns, E. M., 65–66, 73–74, 78, 83–85

Cage, J., 95, 114
Cam, P., 135–139
Categorical perception, 66, 73–75, 78–79,
    84. *See also* Continuous perception
  vs. continuous perception, 74
  defined, 73
Cavell, S., 1, 4–6, 33–35, 37–38, 40–41, 60,
    62, 91–94, 99, 153n6
Chomsky, N., 15–17, 26, 46, 56
Churchland, P. M., 38, 39
Churchland, P. S., 125
C-intervals, 65–66, 70–75, 80–81, 83–85,
    144, 154n6
Clarke, E. F., 55
Cognitivism, 3
Collingwood, R. G., 42
Communication
  linguistic, 41, 54
  musical, 55
Competence
  linguistic, 17, 45–46, 48
  musical, 18, 27–28, 35, 58
  vs. performance, 18, 27, 35 (*see also* Real-
    time processing)
Compliance-classes, 100–103, 105–106,
    108, 119–120, 122
Connectionism, 9, 69
Consciousness, 6, 13, 19, 27, 32, 34–35, 37,
    39, 49–50, 67, 72, 125–145. *See also*
    Qualia

Consonance, vs. dissonance, 24, 51, 52
Continuous perception. *See also* Categori-
    cal perception
  defined, 74
C-pitches, 64–65, 69, 70, 72, 79, 80–83, 87,
    88, 93, 105, 122, 140, 144

Davies, J. B., 7
Dennett, D. C., 5, 9, 125–131, 134–139, 142,
    144–145
Density, in Goodman's *Languages of Art*, 5,
    101–104, 106–108, 110–113, 115–122
  defined, 101–102
Dependent meaning, 45, 57
Determinables, vs. determinates, 65, 116.
    See also Determinates
Determinates, 86, 89, 107–108, 116–117,
    128, 134–135, 140–143. *See also*
    Determinables
Dewey, J., 2, 97
Dickie, G., 10
Differentiation, in Goodman's *Languages
    of Art*, 104–108, 110, 112–113, 115, 118,
    120, 121–122
  defined, 100–103
Dispositions, 159n5
Dowling, W. J., 42
Drake, C., 90
Dummett, M., 118

Emotions, 2, 42, 44, 51, 54, 56–60
  aesthetic emotion, 56, 60
Exemplification, musical, 87, 89, 104, 109–
    110, 112, 113–114, 120, 158n10
Expectancies, musical, 28, 70–71, 76–78
Expectation, semantic, 41, 44–45
Explanation, 2–3, 147n2
Expression, musical. *See* Exemplification

Feeling ineffability, 4, 40, 61, 95
  defined, 38–40
Feelings. *See* Emotions; Musical feelings
Fodor, J. A., 4–5, 8–9, 11–15, 26–27, 54, 63,
  81, 97, 99

Gabrielsson, A., 55, 90
Gardner, H., 11, 15
Global levels of representation, 24, 31–35,
  39, 51. *See also* Local levels of represen-
  tation
Goodman, N., 4–5, 42, 83, 99–123

Hanslick, E., 56
Hardin, C. L., 89
Haugeland, J., 120
Hevner, K., 56
Hierarchical representations, 17, 22, 24–
  25, 50–51, 69
Higgins, K. M., 44
Horrocks, G., 46, 48

Independent meaning, 45–46, 56–58
Inference, perceptual, 11–13, 26
Input systems, 8, 11–15, 26, 81

Jackendoff, R., 4, 8, 15–19, 24–30, 37, 43–
  44, 49–50, 52, 68
Jackson, F., 125
JND. *See* Just noticeable difference
Jones, M. R., 77, 90
Jordan, D. S., 70–71, 78, 84
Judgments. *See* Propositional episodes
Just noticeable difference, 85, 121

Kant, I., 6, 61
Kelly, W. J., 74
Kennick, W. E., 6
Kidd, G., 77
Kivy, P., 43
Knowledge
  knowledge$_d$, 93–95, 147n9
  knowledge$_{sp}$, 91, 93–96, 147n9
  musical, 6, 37
  occurrent, 4, 62, 88–94
Kraut, R., 50, 53, 57
Kuhns, R., 42

Langer, S. K., 1, 6, 35, 40, 42
Lerdahl, F., 4, 8, 15–19, 24–30, 37, 43–44,
  49–50, 52, 68
L-grammar. *See* Linguistic grammar

Linguistic creativity, 16, 46, 54, 56–57
Linguistic grammar, 16, 24, 26, 28, 49
Local levels of representation, 24, 31–35,
  39
  vs. global levels, 24

Marr, D., 42, 120
Memory, 11, 14, 38, 40, 68–70, 73, 80–81,
  84, 86, 88–89, 92–94, 96, 121, 129, 140,
  141, 155n12. *See also* Schemas
Mental score, 64–72, 79, 113, 140, 143
  derivation from N-level, 68–72
Metzler, J., 130
M-grammar. *See* Musical grammar
Modularity, 14
Moore, B. C., 7
Musical feelings, 37, 39, 41, 42, 44, 49–59,
  61
  vs. emotions, 56–60
Musical grammar, 8, 18–19, 24, 26–28, 30–
  31, 34, 49–51, 64–65, 67–68, 122
Musical pitch. *See* Pitch

Nagel, T., 125
Network models, 68, 70, 79, 80, 140
N-intervals, 66–67, 72, 73, 75, 83–86, 89,
  122, 126, 135, 142–143
  defined, 66
N-level, 67–68, 70–72, 83–86, 89–90, 113,
  121, 126, 135–136, 139–140, 143
  defined, 67
Nonstructural features of music, 29, 61–
  62, 90 (*see also* Structural features)
Normativity, 57–60
Notation markings, in Goodman's
  Languages of Art, 103–107, 109–110, 112,
  115, 119
N-pitches, 65, 67, 72, 75, 83, 86–90, 108,
  110, 112, 122, 135, 140–144
  defined, 65
Nuance ineffability, 4, 5, 61, 75, 88, 90, 93,
  95, 113, 115, 126, 144
  defined, 86
Nuances, 4–5, 29, 33, 55, 65–67, 122, 156n4.
  See also N-intervals; N-pitches

Ostension, 88–89, 92–93, 130, 145

Palmer, C., 29, 33, 55, 90
Performance. *See* Competence; Real-time
  processing
Perfect pitch, defined, 154n1

Perlmutter, D. M., 46–48
Phenomenology, 50, 57, 125-145. *See also* Qualia
Picasso, 94
Pips, 132–134
Pitch, defined, 7–8
Prall, D., 157n7, 157n9
Propositional episodes, 5, 126–127, 130, 135
Psychoacoustic correlates, 14, 26, 27

Qualia, 9, 125–126, 130–132, 142–145
Quasi-semantics, musical, 41–42, 51, 53, 55, 61

Raw feels. *See* Qualia
Real-time processing, of music, 3, 18, 24, 27–31, 35, 39, 64–67, 74–79, 90, 121. *See also* Competence
Report, of structural features of music, 31–35, 79–82. *See also* Structural ineffability
Riley, T., 114

Samples, in Goodman's *Languages of Art*. *See* Exemplification
Schank, R. C., 68
Schemas, 14, 25, 40, 61, 68–72, 75, 78, 80–89, 95, 121–123, 125–126, 136, 140, 141, 143. *See also* Memory
  defined, 68
Schopenhauer, A., 42
Scruton, R., 42, 57, 58
Seashore, C., 8, 85
Shepard, R. N., 70–71, 78, 130
Siegal J. A., 74–76
Soames, S., 46–48
Sound-events, in Goodman's *Languages of Art*, 104–112, 116, 119, 121–122
Stoeckig, K., 76
Stravinsky, I., 35, 37, 45, 53
Structural description
  linguistic, 14, 17, 41
  musical, 18–19, 25, 27, 28–29, 31, 33–35, 37, 40, 49, 51, 59, 67, 96, 135
Structural features of music. *See also* Nonstructural features
  defined, 25
  vs. nonstructural features, 25
Structural ineffability, 4, 32, 35
  defined, 32
Supplementary markings, in Goodman's

Languages of Art, 105–113, 115, 118–119, 121–122
Supplemented prolongational reduction, defined, 29
Symbol scheme, in Goodman's *Languages of Art*, defined, 157n2
Symbol system, in Goodman's *Languages of Art*, defined, 157n2

Tonal music, 4, 15, 18, 24–25, 27, 30, 49, 54, 64, 68–70, 72, 76–78, 83–86, 93, 115, 121–122, 135, 144
  vs. atonal music, 70, 78
Transducers, defined, 148n3

Uncertainty, of a stimulus, 65–66, 73–74, 76, 78, 154n6

Vibrato, defined, 154n4

Ward, W. D., 65–66, 73–74, 78, 83–84
Watson, C. S., 74
Wittgenstein, L., 82

Yee, W., 77